Vanessa

Thank you so
your help and support in getting
this written. Evelyn + Louise
xx.

Thriving Abroad

The definitive guide to professional and personal relocation success

Louise Wiles & Evelyn Simpson

First published in Great Britain by
Practical Inspiration Publishing, 2017

© Louise Wiles and Evelyn Simpson, 2017

The moral rights of the authors have been asserted.

ISBN (print): 978-1-910056-57-8
ISBN (ebook): 978-1-910056-56-1

All rights reserved. This book or any portion thereof may not be reproduced without the express written permission of the authors.

 Practical Inspiration
PUBLISHING

Praise for Thriving Abroad

'This book is an important new resource in the toolbox of HR and other relocation specialists. As we give our relocated staff the opportunity of new career paths, new skills and at the same time allow spouses and dependents to fill their own roles within the process, "information is power" and this book includes powerful information.'

Bud Chapman, Welfare Officer,
CfBT Education Services, Brunei Darussalam

'As we are preparing to return home after 3 years in a host country, I wish I had known some of the questions to ask that Louise and Evelyn write about. The single biggest realisation in this journey is that none of us are alone. Wherever you are going and for whatever reason, someone else has been there before, so listen to the lessons in this book and make them part of your journey.'

Pam Barmby, SAHM, South Africa

'Everything you need to know about the practical pitfalls of that job move abroad in one place.'

Peter Ferrigno, former Global Mobility Partner, EY

'After reading this book you will know what you don't know now! Being an expat is a great experience in life but starting to live as an expat is quite a challenge. This book will help you to address all the issues and make your stay abroad a success. Don't be discouraged. Your preparation is a lot of work. Louise and Evelyn are the experts helping you!'

Carine Bormans, expat for 30 years and
coach for expat families

'This is a rare book among a wide variety of books on global mobility. *Thriving Abroad* focuses on making the right decision and your preparation. You can read it before going to whatever country. It is just as important whether moving to Germany or Oman. The book provides you with all the questions you need to prepare well. There is a direct link between your preparation and how well you settle in. Read and use the book and it will become – as the title says – a guide to relocation success.'

Lena Lauridsen, consultant and
author of two books on relocation

'It's an indispensable read for the assignees and their partners, a book to keep handy in the messiest moment of a family's life. With its check lists and adaptation strategies, it's a great tool for coping with rationality and order to change and transition.'

Marta Guarneri, expat with 20 years of experience both as assignee and partner

'If you are considering an overseas assignment this excellent resource will quickly become your handbook. Offering comprehensive, accessible advice on all aspects of ensuring that your life abroad will be as successful and happy as possible, it will prompt you to consider and discuss the many important decisions to be made that can often be rushed or overlooked in the excitement and chaos that international relocation can bring. Whether you are just considering a move, are in the throes of planning or have recently arrived and are deep in culture shock, this book provides balanced and reassuring advice that you will undoubtedly find helpful.'

Vanessa Dennet, expat partner

'I wish this book had been written sixteen years ago when we first relocated; it could have saved us learning a lot of lessons the hard way! This book will prove invaluable for anyone considering an overseas move and will help them organize their thoughts in what can be an entirely overwhelming process.'

Suzanna Standring, Chartered Accountant, USA

'*Thriving Abroad* superbly manages a difficult task. It takes a difficult, emotionally loaded topic; collects the best research and knowledge around the subject; and collates it all in a very comprehensive, practical guide. It does all of that in a user-friendly tone and format laced with anecdote, so the intimidating topic becomes easy to read. This is going to be my go-to, well thumbed through reference book for our next move. I'll be carrying it with me everywhere!'

Maryam Afnan Ahmad, co-author Slurping Soup and Other Confusions, *teacher, trainer*

Contents

Foreword

*'It is beyond a doubt that all our knowledge
begins with experience.'*
Immanuel Kant

I fully subscribe to this timeless observation of the late German philosopher. After my education in Germany I worked in India, Turkey, the Czech Republic and Switzerland. I do not regret any of the experiences I had in these countries. Of course, there were challenging situations, but they made me who I am today.

During my career, spanning over 20 years, I have advised more than 100 companies in 34 countries and assisted their mobility functions to become more strategic and to do a better job for their most important stakeholders, the international assignees and their families.

My personal experience of living and working in different countries and cultures helps me relate to my work as a strategic global mobility adviser. Having relocated on a range of different bases – as a Local Plus in India, a Euro commuter to Turkey and a fully fledged expat in the Czech Republic before finally being localized into Switzerland – I understand the decisions that companies take in defining the employee experience. Mobility strategies, policies, delivery models: all these elements have a great impact on the employee experience of an assignee and his or her family.

I have drawn two key insights from my experience. First, it's important to acknowledge the decision-making process and culture. Most of the decisions in mobility departments are based on four distinct criteria: cost, risk, complexity and attractiveness. Second, both country *and* company culture shape the employee experience. Depending on the company culture, the above four criteria will be weighed differently.

Assignees and their families tend to care most about attractiveness and minimized risk for themselves, while the corporate seeks to balance the different points of view by taking all four criteria into consideration.

If human resources staff were athletes, mobility would be the decathlon. International assignment management is one of the most complex areas within human resources. Consider the following points.

- Compliance requirements for tax, social security, immigration, labour law and travel security not only differ from country to country, but are constantly changing.
- Normally HR would not be engaged in the family and housing situation of local employees, but the employee's personal situation becomes relevant when he or she is sent on an international assignment. Once HR extends to global mobility, it has to be involved in these personal issues.

The mobility functions themselves are facing a time of change. From an assignee perspective, this is good news. Increasingly they are regarding compliance as a hygiene factor (something that won't make you happy but needs to be done – think of work permit administration or kidnap training) and are beginning to shift their focus more towards the employee experience and towards a purpose-driven rationale for global mobility.

The true purpose of a modern mobility function should be to enable assignees and their families to achieve a smooth international relocation. This will facilitate the assignees' engagement, performance, and development and ultimately their successful repatriation and reintegration, all the while ensuring that their families also enjoy meaningful and positive life experiences abroad.

Many mobility functions face an uphill battle. They must define their strategic choices based on multiple stakeholders, strategy and business objectives and market trends and challenges, as well as on company culture. One tip from my side for assignees would be that trying to understand the mobility function (decathletes!) and their challenges better will generate more positive experiences for both sides. This book will help assignees to do just that.

An international assignment is undisputedly one of the most significant experiences an employee can have during his or her career. It involves entire families, and working in other cultural contexts creates great learning and developmental opportunities. But it also involves risks: life stress, family separation, and potential career uncertainty and reintegration challenges on repatriation.

The book aims to encourage a proactive approach in which preparation, forward thinking and shared purpose are key. These things provide the foundation for a smoother adjustment and for better employee engagement and performance.

If I regret one thing about my international experience, it would be that back then, there was no such book to help me avoid the negative experiences and build strategies to maximize the opportunity an international assignment brings.

Chris Debner
Strategic Global Mobility Advisory LLC
Zurich, Switzerland
www.chrisdebner.com

A note from the authors

'It always seems impossible until it is done.'
Nelson Mandela

Welcome to the world of global mobility. A world of new beginnings filled with anticipation, excitement, discovery and opportunity. One where differences are celebrated, cultures co-exist and lifelong relationships are formed in both the professional and personal worlds.

This is a world where the person you are today represents the foundation of who you will become tomorrow. Should you decide to embark on this international journey, you must prepare to be challenged personally and professionally in every way. The payoff? A wealth of opportunity in terms of experiences and personal growth.

This book started with a journey – an adventure, if you like. Not that either of us thought of it in that way when we both embarked on our lives abroad over 20 years ago. We left family, friends and jobs and started new lives. The experiences that followed have led us to where we are today, writing this book, and therein lies another surprise: we never imagined we would write a book!

Looking back, we wouldn't change any of our major decisions and we don't regret our journeys, but we know that if we had our time again, we would do certain things differently.

Our roles as coaches have enabled us to reflect on our experiences; the learning and insights are what we share in this book. But this is not all. We also link our lessons and insights to the context of global mobility. Global mobility, at its best, works with the big-picture macro view of international strategy and global talent management while managing the micro perspective of the individuals whose lives are impacted in every way by that strategy. Global mobility professionals *do* the work in facilitating the international relocation process; employees and their families *live it*. In this book we seek to connect the two.

International relocation is not a simple house move or job change. The decision you make will affect your life in every conceivable way, and yet often it is portrayed as an exercise in practical transition. A job is offered, which happens to be abroad. A support package and salary is agreed. Flights are booked, accommodation sorted and boxes packed. One location is switched to another and off you go, into the sunset and the life of happily ever after.

How we wish that were always true!

While many people say that their lives have been enriched by their international experience and that they wouldn't change their fundamental decision to give it a try, we know there are often trials and tribulations along the way.

Why?

Because international relocation involves the relocation of *you*, and you are more than a physical location and a lorry load of cardboard boxes. You relocate with hopes, dreams, expectations and feelings. Relocation is as much a psychological transition as it is a practical one. It is also a change process, one that affects every aspect of your life.

Whatever the pull to your new life abroad, there will be days when you question your decision, and when you wonder about its impact on your loved ones. You may sometimes ask, 'Can I really do this?'

At those times, it will help to know that you are not the only one to feel like this. It will be comforting to know that you went into the process consciously and with your eyes wide open. It will help to know that your decision and preparation created the best possible foundation on which to build your success.

The world of business is becoming ever more global. The future expansion of international businesses depends on people like you who have the drive and desire for adventure and for developing mutually beneficial relationships in this ever more connected world.

This book is designed to support you through the process, from decision to the creation of a thriving and successful life abroad for everyone involved in the move.

We wish you all the luck in the world!

Acknowledgements

A book is never the sole production of its authors. It is the compilation of experiences, ideas and insights generated from research and many conversations. We would like to thank:

- the global mobility and HR professionals who so generously gave their time and shared their experience of and vision for global mobility in the 21st century;
- our book reviewers who generously gave their time to read and provide such thorough and constructive feedback;
- the Thriving Abroad podcast interviewees for their insights and generosity in sharing their international experiences and learnings;
- the professionals who shared their expertise – Lucy Greenwood of the International Family Law Group; Caron Pope, Managing Partner of Fragomen Worldwide; Neil Long of Bond Dickinson; Alison Hesketh of Time Finders, Rita Rosenback of Multilingual Parenting; Rachel Yates of Expat Lifeline; Tim Wells, Partner at Abbis Cadres; Liz Perelstein of School Choice International; and Padraig O'Sullivan of O'Sullivanfield – contact details can be found in the resources section of this book;
- Chris Debner, for writing the foreword and positioning our book and its support for the assignee in the context of global mobility so eloquently;
- those whose experience and story we shared directly – Jacquie Kane, Josephine Ryan, Chantal Duke and Kristin Louise Duncombe;
- our clients, friends and colleagues for inviting us into their lives and allowing us to be a part of their journeys; their lives, experiences and insights have been truly inspiring and helped to inform the content of this book;
- all the contributors to our survey Career Choice and the Accompanying Partner (2012); they inspired us to move forward with the creation of Thriving Abroad and writing this book;

- Karen Williams of Librotas Books for getting us into action – for getting the book outline out of our heads and onto paper;
- Alison Jones, our publisher, for the fabulous proposal-writing workshop that connected us with you; for demonstrating your belief in us and our book and publishing it; and, of course, for your expert guidance through the editing, publishing and marketing process;
- our copy-editor, Rachel Small, and project manager, Anke Ueberberg;
- our friends who have supported and cheered us along the way;
- our colleagues at Families in Global Transitions; what a fantastic organization – one which inspired us to write a book that speaks to both the practicalities and the lived experience of international relocation; and
- last, but not least, our families, particularly our long-suffering husbands and children. The book has been a feature of all our lives for perhaps a bit too long; your love, support and patience has meant the world.

Who and how?

'True wisdom is knowing what you don't know.'
Confucius

Who this book is for

This book is for anyone who has ever considered relocating internationally through their organization. While focused on the corporate sector, much of the content is relevant whether you are relocating with a multinational, a non-profit or a government organization.

The book is written for the potential or imminent assignee and their partner. We have written it in this way because we believe that the decision to relocate internationally should be a joint one; a decision made consultatively and based on a foundation of solid research and understanding of the challenges and opportunities of international relocation. We envisage that both partners will read this book and use it as their personal guide to international relocation success. We encourage you to discuss your individual motivations and concerns for international relocation openly, to search together for the shared purpose and reason behind making such a life-changing decision and to aim to achieve the best possible fit between personal and professional aspirations for both partners.

This book is for you whether you work for an organization that sees international mobility as an important part of its talent strategy or an organization that has the occasional international opportunity. Perhaps you have been included in an assignment pool, have been asked whether you are interested in a specific international role, have been offered an international position, or simply wonder whether this is something for you, one day. You may have questions about the potential career value of an international move; you may wonder about the challenges and whether the opportunities and benefits of a broader life perspective will be worthwhile.

As the accompanying partner, you recognize that a move for your partner's career will have a significant impact on your life personally and professionally. Of course, you want to better understand the potential implications of such a move. These thoughts may be further complicated if you have children.

Assignee or partner, you may be struggling with making the definitive relocation decision, yes or no. You need some assistance in thinking it all through. After all, it is an important decision, perhaps one of the most important you have ever had to make. What must you consider and weigh up to make an informed and joint decision?

Decision made, then there are the logistical challenges. Just thinking about the physical move raises your heart rate! You recognize that it is important that you prepare well. But where to start? You also want to secure the best possible support from your organization, but having never relocated abroad, you have no certainty about what that support could look like.

And what about the longer term? You have seen people benefit greatly from gaining international experience and observed others struggling with disappointing longer term career outcomes. How can you ensure the longer term positive career outcome for yourself?

This book sets out to help you to answer all these questions and more. While we cannot make the decision for you, we can help you to make your decision based on a solid understanding of the potential benefits, opportunities and challenges of international living.

This book is also for those who are already well into their international journey. You may have worked your way through the relocation process a couple of times already, but these pages will offer more useful tips and advice, different perspectives and encouraging stories. And of course, in the international mobility world there is always another decision to be made at some point. Chapter Five will help you to nail that.

How to use this book

This book is structured around the Framework for Thriving Abroad, which is presented in the introduction and guides you through the cycle of international relocation. An international move is about more than the movement of you and your belongings from one location to another. It is about managing change from both a practical and psychological perspective – change that potentially impacts every aspect of your life. This book supports you from both perspectives.

The book does not make the relocation decision for you. Neither does it tell you explicitly what to do. Through sharing experiences, stories, insights and advice, this book aims to give you a feel for what it means to live and work abroad. Questions are designed to prompt thought and action and lead you to managing your potential international experience in the best way possible for you and your family.

Throughout the book you will see 'Reflection time' and this icon ☼. At these points, we will ask you a question that links to a section in a workbook that you can access online through the Thriving Abroad website. You have not just purchased a book to read – you have also purchased access to the accompanying workbook and podcast interviews in which expats share experiences and advice. To access these, go to the Thriving Abroad website: www.ThrivingAbroad.com/Book. When prompted, insert the password 'Decision'.

How this book is structured

Part One is all about laying the foundation for making an informed decision based on sound research and understanding of the context, challenges and opportunities of global mobility and international relocation.

Part Two is about preparing in the best possible way for the transition to your new life abroad. There is much to do from a practical perspective, and we guide you through the most important 'must dos' with tips and suggestions to ease the workload. But practical preparation is only half the story. Transition and change has an emotional impact, which needs to be acknowledged and managed; Part Two handles this aspect of relocation as well.

Part Three is about building your fulfilling and successful life abroad. Arriving and unpacking the boxes is not the end of the change process; in fact, it is more the beginning. Adjustment can be a roller-coaster experience, and Part Three supports you in building strategies to minimize the negative effects of change. Beyond the adjustment process, Part Three focuses on how you can create a *thriving* professional and personal life abroad, and looks forward to the next phase of your international journey.

The book can be read from beginning to end. Reading it this way will be particularly helpful for anyone wanting to gain an overall sense of the experience of international relocation and whether it is right for them. It can also be used part by part to support you through the relocation process as you live it and move through each stage of your international move.

Introduction

'While it's wise to learn from experience, it's wiser to learn from the experiences of others.'[1]

Rick Warren

Welcome

Relocating internationally will affect pretty much every aspect of your life, from what you eat and where you buy food to your sense of safety and security and your basic level of comfort in terms of housing and daily living. Your social and professional networks will change and evolve as you leave behind established connections and strive to build new ones. You will adjust to the new culture and language and adapt to the new living and working environment and organizational culture. For the partner who is leaving a career behind, the absence of a professional role can lead to existential challenges and questions.

We have heard expats talk about the privilege of their lives in one breath, and the challenges in the next. It can be an eclectic experience – one that challenges and inspires in multiple ways leading to varied reactions from different family members at different times.

Many people have faced and overcome these challenges to build lives abroad that are rich in terms of experience and personal and professional development. Many say that they do not regret relocating internationally but believe it could have been an easier process. Consider the following situations, which may exacerbate the challenges:

- An urgent business need requires an employee to relocate rapidly. The employee must make quick decisions based on insufficient knowledge and understanding of the role, location and potential challenges involved.
- The employee has no previous international experience. If someone has never relocated abroad, he or she may have a limited awareness of

the potential challenges, the preparation required or the adjustment process that relocation entails.

- The move abroad is seen through rose-tinted spectacles. Naturally, we tend to view the future optimistically and overestimate the likelihood of positive events happening in the future while underestimating the likelihood of negative events. This 'optimism bias' can lead us to imagine life will be better and fail to consider the associated risks and challenges.[2]
- The decision is based on the employee's role and the organization's need for him or her to fill a role abroad. The needs of the partner and family are not adequately considered. They are simply expected to follow too.

While the need for quick decisions cannot always be avoided, we believe it is important to make your decision and relocation preparations based on an understanding of the experience you are undertaking. This book gives you a sense of that experience and then guides you through the relocation process. It helps you to prepare well by laying the foundations for a happy and fulfilling life abroad.

The aim is to:

- give you comprehensive insight into the relocation experience, detailing the good, the bad and the ugly;
- guide you in your research of the location, challenges and opportunities so that you know what to expect and can relocate with realistic expectations;
- encourage you to make an informed decision based on an understanding of the purpose and value of the relocation experience for all family members. This informed decision will form the foundation of your preparation for your move abroad, should you decide to go;
- guide your preparation from a practical and psychological perspective; and
- encourage you to be proactive in your preparation and your ownership of the experience and successful outcome.

We provide tips and suggestions and share stories of success and failure. We want to give you a sense of the experience you are planning to undertake. As Marta Guarneri, one of our reviewers and an expat with 20 years of experience both as assignee and partner, said: 'Readers will find this book very valuable as it provides them with the questions they have no experiences to know the importance of.'

Throughout the book we prompt your research and contemplation with questions. Remember to download the accompanying workbook from www.ThrivingAbroad.com/book. When prompted, insert the password 'Decision'.

Now we'll introduce you to two of the core elements contained in this book: two case studies, which will make regular appearances, and the Framework for Thriving Abroad, which describes the relocation process and highlights its five key stages. Below each chapter heading, a diagram of the framework will highlight where the chapter content fits into the relocation process.

Case studies

Throughout the book you will follow the international journey of two families. These are not real-life families; we are not compromising the confidentiality of any of our clients, friends, or colleagues. We have created their stories by drawing from our personal experience and observation of hundreds of expats around the world.

These case studies are designed to bring to life the advice, insights, and observations in this book. There's nothing like a good story, after all.

Jenny and Paul

Jenny, 38, and Paul, 40, relocated to Shanghai, China, from the UK three years ago. They moved together with their two children, James and Susie, aged eight and six respectively. They had never lived abroad before but had been hoping for an opportunity to do so for the past two years – in fact, Paul had been actively looking for a role abroad. Therefore, it was a real surprise when the opportunity arose for Jenny. She was offered a position in a global media agency in Shanghai, a subsidiary of a parent company that she worked for in the UK. Initially they were torn. They had always imagined it would be Paul's job that would lead the way.

Paul was unsure he wanted to leave his role in the UK. Though people told him it would be possible to find work in China, there was no certainty. And he was unsure how he felt about being a stay-at-home dad. In some ways it was an attractive proposition. He'd have time to focus on the children and his interests and hobbies. But Paul had always valued his career and the contribution he made. As he and Jenny discussed the opportunity, he realized that a short-term career break would be helpful in the initial stages as they settled themselves and their children into their new lives. He hoped after the settling-in phase he would be able to find work.

Jenny was simultaneously excited at the prospect of the new role and worried at the thought of potentially becoming the sole income generator for the family. Having only ever visited China on work trips, she wondered how it would be to live there. What would the schooling options be for the children? How would the children feel about moving such a long way from home, their friends and grandparents? Overriding all these concerns, for both Paul and Jenny, there was a feeling of anticipation and excitement. This was a chance to try something completely new, to realize their dream of living abroad.

Rich and Angela

Rich, 30, and Angela, 32, relocated to the UK two years ago. Up until this point they had lived in the USA all their lives but loved travelling. If they weren't on holiday they were planning their next trip; they had a long list of countries they wanted to visit. Living abroad was not something they had ever considered in any detail. It was something they chatted about over a glass of wine on holiday while imagining their retirement – one day! Their life was good. They had no children (yet) but a great circle of friends. Their comfortable little bubble was burst when out of the blue Rich's company asked him to consider relocating to head the European finance team in London. Rich was so thrilled that the company had identified him for this role that he almost said yes on the spot. He stopped himself in the nick of time to suggest that he would get back to them in a few days after speaking to Angela. Rich was certain she would be thrilled – after all, who wouldn't want to live in London? Okay, she would have to leave her job, but she'd never given the impression that she was that committed to it. And who knew what work opportunities would await her in London.

To his surprise, Angela was less than enthusiastic. In fact, for the first 30 minutes of their conversation she said almost nothing, just listened as he explained the role and how pleased he was to have been offered it. Looking for ways to enthuse Angela, Rich drew on the location – they could travel and tour around amazing European cities, places it would have taken them years to work their way around from the US. Now they could hop onto planes and trains and be there within hours. Weekends would be great. Angela began to feel a little more excited by the prospect.

Putting yourselves in the shoes of these two couples, what would you want to know about the opportunity before making the decision, yes or no?

Introducing the Framework for Thriving Abroad

International relocation involves big changes – changes that affect not only the assignee's work role but also the personal and family life of the assignee and partner.

The Framework for Thriving Abroad demonstrates this dynamic change process.

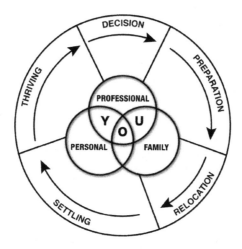

Framework for Thriving Abroad

In the following section the framework is explained.

Working from the outside in

International relocation is a process of change and transition, and is represented here by the arrows in the framework.

Let's start by looking at the headline segments of this process. First, a *decision* is made. It may be driven by the organization, the employee/family, or both. The way in which the decision is made is important as this will lay the foundation for the assignment experience. The best decisions are given some time and involve the assignee, partner and organization.

After the decision is made to embark on an international relocation assignment, there is then a period of *preparation*; professional and personal, practical and emotional. While we can never rule out all surprises, there are positive ways to prepare both practically and emotionally that will create a smoother adjustment process.

Preparation is followed by the physical *relocation*, which initiates a period of transition and adjustment, or *settling in*. This can be a challenging time for all members of the family at different times, and is often punctuated by a succession of highs and lows as each person adjusts to the new environments. While it would be wrong to suggest that there is an absolute end to the adjustment process, over time, people begin to feel more settled and able to focus on creating happy, fulfilling, and *thriving* lives in their new locations.

Relocation is a dynamic process with one relocation leading to another, even if it is a move back home. Wherever the next move is, and this includes repatriation, there is always another process of change and transition to be worked through.

International assignment at its very essence is a change process from both a personal and professional perspective. Every aspect of your life will change as you relocate.

The environment and culture in which you are living will change, as will the people with whom you interact. Your professional and personal roles will change. As the assignee, your role in the workplace environment will be different to your home country role. You may become the sole provider in your family. As the partner, you may take on a new role abroad or leave your career behind and stop working outside the home for a while, perhaps take on voluntary roles. You may become dependent on your partner financially for the first time in your life and find that these changes affect your sense of who you are – your personal identity. If you have children, they will need to adjust to the new general, cultural and school environments.

Assignee or partner, you will need to adjust to these changing roles, relationships and responsibilities as well as the new environment, language and culture. You will need to make emotional and psychological adjustments. Adjustment generally does not have a start and end-by date. It is a process that continues to have an impact at different points and levels over time.

For the assignee, your work life will become more complex. As you consider your relocation decision and subsequent preparation, you will liaise with connections in your organization who will influence and manage your relocation experience. As you manage the transition process, you will liaise between the home management and host country management teams, who will define your role and manage your arrival. There will also be a range of personnel and global mobility managers involved in managing all aspects of your relocation, from your contract, to visas, to the physical move. It can be a complicated exercise in effective communication and relationship management. This is because everyone has a role to play in influencing the outcome of the assignment.

- The company will have an interest in the role – in its purpose, its value and your ability to perform in it. The company will also be interested in bringing about the relocation as cost efficiently as possible.
- As the assignee, you will have an interest in the role – in its purpose and value in terms of income, experience and career development. You will also be interested in the experience from a broader life perspective.
- Your partner and family will have a vested interest in the whole experience. They will, initially at least, be dependent on you and your company to support them through this life-changing experience.
- As the partner of an assignee, you may be leaving a career and role in your home country. You will need to manage your exit from that while organizing your physical relocation and perhaps a job search or your integration into a new work role abroad.

Everyone involved will have a different agenda. The challenge will be to coordinate these different interests and motivations so that they all interact in a positive and cohesive way.

Both assignee and partner will be managing relationships with children, extended family members, and friends. This can be a bittersweet time as you recognize the importance of these relationships and confront the reality that the nature of your relationships will change.

At the heart of the circle is **YOU**. Assignee or partner, your presence at centre of the mobility circle emphasizes that international relocation will affect every area of your life: your working life, your personal life, and your family life. Gaining clarity on your motives for a life change as big as international relocation is an important first step in the adjustment process that will lead to the creation of a *thriving* life abroad. Finding a balance between the three areas of your life will also be important. Each affects the other, and roles in the three areas can expand and contract over time.

Around the framework we have four important questions that we will return to throughout the book: What? Why? How? and Who?

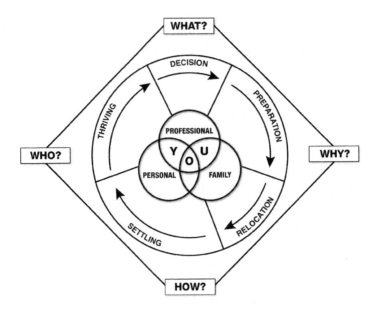

What?

This question prompts you to consider *what* international relocation will mean to you from a professional, personal and family perspective. It is helpful to understand:

- the opportunities, benefits and challenges of international relocation. This understanding will enable you to better manage the adjustment process and create strategies to minimize or even eliminate some challenges and set more realistic expectations, while simultaneously recognizing the opportunities and benefits of the experience;
- what matters most to you in terms of what you want to experience and achieve from the relocation abroad; and
- what support needs and expectations you have and how well your organization will meet them.

Why?

This is about understanding the motivation behind what you choose to do in life. To uncover your why, think about what matters most to you in all areas of your life. This will help you to identify your personal and professional values. What is your 'reason why' for moving abroad in relation to your:

- work and professional life;
- personal life; and
- family life.

Gaining clarity on your why is very important when making your relocation decision and in providing the foundation for a successful transition.

We will revisit this very important question in Chapter Five.

How?

There is a dual perspective to the question *how*. The first relates to the practicalities, the second to making the experience a success for all concerned.

How will you make it happen?

Relocating abroad will require a lot of planning and preparation. How? Will become a familiar question as you secure a position abroad and plan your move.

How will you make it a success?

You will utilize your personal and professional skills, strengths and knowledge to build your success in your career and life abroad. There are many skills and much knowledge that will help you to relocate successfully and thrive abroad. How aware are you of your skill set and personal strengths? How will those skills and knowledge support you through the transition experience? Perhaps you have a knack for learning languages, or you're great at networking. Maybe you have managed yourself and others through big change programmes.

It is also a good time to think about where you may lack knowledge or skills and seek professional support to help you in developing that knowledge.

Who?

We are social beings and we need social connection and support to thrive. Our networks and connections, relationships and attachments are important in supporting us and helping us to deliver on both professional and personal goals. They support us in achieving personal and professional success.

Relationships and the social support derived from them will ease the adjustment process. Think about the networks that you have already and can develop; think about new networks you can create in both your home and your host location that will support you through the transition experience.

Summary

- ❑ Relocating internationally will affect every aspect of your life.
- ❑ We've introduced you to our two case studies; their experiences and stories will appear throughout the book.

❑ This book guides you through the relocation process. The five stages of relocation are highlighted in the Framework for Thriving Abroad:
- ◆ Decision
- ◆ Preparation
- ◆ Relocation
- ◆ Settling
- ◆ Thriving

❑ Gaining an understanding of the context, challenges and opportunities of global mobility is an important part of making an informed decision.

❑ There are four important questions: What? Why? How? and Who? We will return to these regularly throughout the book; they'll guide your research, preparation and adjustment.

PART ONE

Putting International Relocation into Context

CHAPTER ONE

Gearing up for success

'If everyone is moving forward together, then success takes care of itself.'
Henry Ford

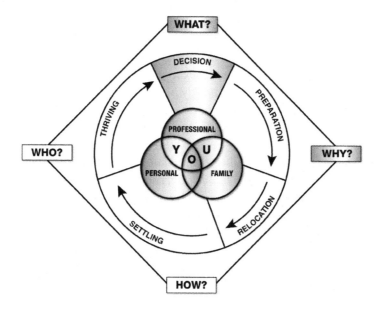

Jenny and Paul

As she sank into her comfy airport lounge sofa, glass of wine in hand, Jenny felt the stress of packing up begin to drift away. She looked at her children and thought that they looked confident and happy, as did Paul. Yes, despite a rocky start, she felt that she could now say their time in China had been positive, with some notable successes; her job had gone well, and she felt her promotion to the Chinese role had been well deserved. Paul had achieved his MBA and the children, they had loved their time in Shanghai.

Jenny thought back to the conversations they had before leaving for China. Paul had been hesitant about leaving his job. While he recognized it was a great career move for Jenny, he was worried that it would irreparably damage his own. He couldn't envisage a life without a career. Eventually he reasoned that if it provided career progression for Jenny and a great life experience for the family, and if he could ultimately find a professional outlet in China, then it would be an exciting opportunity for everyone. However, on arrival, Paul insisted he needed to find work quickly. He seemed to do an about-turn on his original decision to take a short-term career break. While Jenny was working all hours, settling into her new job, Paul was anxiously scouring the city for work, all the while getting more and more depressed about the lack of appropriate opportunities. He was looking for something that could be flexible around the children, and it quickly became apparent that this wouldn't be easy to find. It all came to a head about seven months in, when Paul announced 'this move' was not working for him. They discussed alternatives and Jenny encouraged Paul to do the MBA he'd always wished he'd done. Things improved dramatically – Paul had found a professional outlet. But, it had been a tough start; Jenny had felt alternately guilty about the situation her career move had put him in, and annoyed at his lack of support for her. She was working all hours and finding her integration into her new role and Chinese culture super challenging. Now, looking back, she recognized these as typical adjustment challenges. Fortunately for both, after the first year, their lives moved forward much more positively..

Introduction

Paul and Jenny had a rough start. It is not unusual to find the first few months challenging; simply settling into a new job can be tough enough without all the challenges related to an international move. For Jenny, the adjustment process was a surprise, and Paul's unrealistic expectations about his employability didn't help, particularly as he wanted to find a role that would give him the flexibility he needed for looking after the children. Fortunately, he found an alternative way of achieving the sense of professional accomplishment that he needed, and the family did settle in and come to enjoy their life in Shanghai.

In this chapter, we encourage you to think about what would constitute success for you, recognizing that this will vary for each family member. Paul's initial job search and success or otherwise looked set to colour their whole experience. Being able to pursue his professional interests in some way was something that mattered to him more than he had expected when initially making the decision to relocate. However, he had to balance that need against those of the rest of the family. They believed that moving abroad would be a great experience for everyone. Paul saw the value of his being at home more for the children and Jenny was excited by the job role and the opportunities it presented for development and promotion. They had a clear view of why this move was important for them from the outset but needed to be flexible and make some adjustments along the way to make it work for everyone.

When relocating internationally it is easy to focus more on the short-term logistics of 'getting there' and, for the assignee, settling into a new role. This is understandable – it is a big upheaval, one that takes a lot of headspace, and settling in well is a laudable short-to-medium-term goal.

But what about longer term? An assignment is for a set term. What is the bigger or longer-term picture? What will determine assignment success from a personal, professional and family perspective three or four years down the line?

What does success mean to you? Success means different things for different people. It is worth thinking about these success factors from the outset. Some may relate to what you achieve while living abroad. Achievements might include meeting your career or role objectives or learning the language, gaining new professional qualifications like Paul, creating new social and professional networks, and happy children who have settled well into their new schools.

Other interpretations of success may relate to experiences you enjoy while abroad. Perhaps these include travelling (in the case of Rich and Angela), spending time together as a family (in the case of Jenny and Paul), and enjoying the culture, food and traditions of your host country. These achievements and experiences all provide an overall sense that the assignment has been a success.

Everyone relocates abroad with a vision; even our friends and families will often hold visions on our behalf. When Louise left the UK to relocate to Madrid, Spain, her colleagues wrote in her leaving card 'Enjoy the sun, sea and sangria'. This statement demonstrated two things. The first was the desperate geographical knowledge of her colleagues! The second was the holiday analogy that is so often connected to international travel. We tend, initially at least, to react to the broad question of international relocation with a vision of what that life could look like – and usually it is a positive picture, which involves leaving our frustrations and troubles behind.

So, in thinking about what you want to create in your new life, it is important to be realistic. Unrealistic expectations can negatively affect the adjustment process.

As we are talking about relocation from the perspective of the corporate sector, it is likely that one element of your desired success will relate to professional outcomes. But personal and family outcomes also matter. It is helpful to think about what success in these three areas might look like to you. To understand what will make the experience a success for you, clarify what is important to you so that you can make plans of action that will help move you forward in those areas once you arrive abroad.

Of course, you cannot anticipate all experiences and successes now. Many factors influence the outcome of international assignments. Some will be beyond your control, such as unforeseeable economic, political and organizational change. However, there are ways in which you, working in collaboration with your organization, can positively influence the outcome of your assignment.

In this chapter, we make some suggestions about what success may look like for you from a personal, professional and family perspective. It is not only your perspective on success that matters. It is important to understand the organization's perspective as well. How does your organization perceive global mobility and its value to the business? How does it monitor the outcomes of international assignment in terms of your contribution and performance?

We conclude the chapter by offering some thoughts on what contributes to creating a life abroad in which you thrive.

Differing perspectives on international assignment success

There are two core perspectives in relation to determining assignment success:

- the perspective of the assignee and the expat partner; and
- the perspective of the organization.

These two broad categories make it sound quite straightforward, but when you consider the people and relationships involved in making an international assignment happen successfully, simplicity can fly out of the window.

Begin to unpack the different perspectives and you will find a complex interaction of factors and relationships that influence not only the definition of what constitutes assignment success, but also the outcome.

Let's take a look at these different perspectives.

What constitutes success in international mobility for the assignee and accompanying partner?

There are many ways to look at success. We suggest you think about it from both the professional and personal perspectives. Here are some ideas to prompt your thoughts.

Personal adjustment to the new environment. To achieve personal and professional satisfaction, you will need to adjust successfully to the new culture, work and general environment. Inability to adjust is one of the most frequently cited reasons for early return. We talk about adjustment challenges and strategies later in the book; for now, simply note it as an important precursor to your ability to engage and perform effectively in your work role and settle into your new life personally.[3]

Job success. You will need to adjust to the new job and work role. Success will relate to your feeling of satisfaction with the role, and to achieving the required level of performance.

Career success. Like Jenny, you may be motivated to relocate due to the career-enhancing potential of the assignment experience. Success in this sense will relate to a combination of objective and subjective outcomes, such as your sense of career satisfaction, possibility for promotion and onward career development, and pay increases.

Development success. One of the key motivations for international assignment is often the developmental opportunity provided by the experience. You will acquire new knowledge, skills and abilities. These will enhance your marketability, either within your current organization or externally. Non-working partners, like Paul, should recognize the value of international relocation as a personal developmental opportunity as well.[4]

The development of new networks and relationships. The international opportunity will enable you to develop new connections both within your organization and within the local and international community. These networks will help you to perform your work roles and develop your future career and will provide personal support.

Personal success factors. While the primary purpose of an international assignment may be the assignee's work role, the whole experience is set within the broader context of personal and family life. What would represent success for you in each of those areas? Think about the hobbies and interests you would like to pursue outside work. How do you envisage spending time with your family?

Partners do not always choose to work while abroad. If you as the partner are thinking that you will not work, or perhaps will be unable to work in the conventional career sense while abroad, what will give you a sense of personal and professional achievement?

What constitutes success for the organization?

International assignment represents a big investment from the organization's perspective. It costs, on average, the equivalent of three times the salary to physically relocate and support an employee. Organizations recognize the value in monitoring return on investment (ROI) in relation to global mobility. However, only 6% of organizations say that they achieve this in any meaningful way.[5] In an Ernst and Young (EY) survey, 72% of corporate contributors said that they do not actually track the outcome of international assignments.[6]

One of the most-cited indications of assignment success is whether the assignment is seen through to the end of its original term, within budget. In the EY survey, where this is assessed, 80% of organizational respondents said seeing assignments through to the end of their terms was a key factor in success.

Using this measure of success, research shows the majority of international assignments appear to be successful, with reports of only 1 in 20 assignments ending in failure and slightly less in early return.[7] Even early return, which is often painted as a negative outcome, may not always be a bad thing when resulting from changing organizational priorities, objectives reached ahead of schedule or from assignee choice as they leave to work elsewhere.

These measures give a pretty positive image of the success of international relocation. The question, though, is whether these are the best measures of assignment success.

Probably not, but it is a complex issue to resolve. International relocation is a multifaceted experience. There are numerous stakeholders with different interests and motivations in the process. Just as the assignee's interest extends beyond the work role to the overall experience of international relocation and its impact on partners and/or family, there will be different expectations regarding positive outcomes from the numerous interested parties to an assignment. Consider the following examples.

- Global mobility may regard a successful assignment as one that stays within budget and is compliant from a tax and legal perspective. Whereas talent management may see it as successful when the assignee is promoted because of their work.

- Assignments that are seen through to the end may be viewed as successful in global mobility terms. But there can still be negative outcomes when the executive returns to their original or a suboptimal position on repatriation, or takes on a suboptimal role in a new location.

- Simply seeing an assignment through to the end of its term within budget does not guarantee positive outcomes. Research has suggested that up to 50% of international assignees who do not return home early underperform in their roles abroad.[8] This statistic is supported by research conducted by Right Management, which found that of 202 CEOs and senior human resources (HR) professionals surveyed, only 42% of assignments were judged as successful.[9]

Desired outcomes therefore may vary for the many interested parties. Most importantly for the assignee, many organizations do not have a handle on the outcomes or ROI generated by their global mobility programmes. This can mean that underperformance issues are masked, but the converse can also be true – good performance may not be recognized.

This makes a powerful argument for developing personal clarity about what will constitute a successful outcome and experience for you and your family from both a personal perspective and a professional one. Developing this clarity is important for many reasons.

- You will be better able to demonstrate success from a work-related perspective. Be vigilant in understanding the role you are relocating to perform, and in how the role's outcomes can best be monitored and measured.

- You will be able to put the international experience into the context of your longer-term life and career vision. Remember that an international assignment is only one relatively short period in your overall lifespan. It is important to keep it in perspective and plan for the longer-term future too. This is particularly important for partners who choose to put careers on hold for one international move.

- You will understand why international relocation is right for you beyond the work-related role.

- You will be prepared for the reality that international relocation affects every aspect of your life. Success is likely to have different meanings for different parts of your life and for different family members.

- You will be able to influence how your organization matches your talents and career objectives with international mobility, leading to a win-win for all.

Reflection time 1.0

What will constitute personal, professional and family success for you should you move abroad?

How will your performance be monitored and assessed by your organization?

What does it mean to thrive abroad?

Some people are attracted to international relocation because it gives them the opportunity for a new episode in their lives. Whether or not you feel this way about it, it does provide an opportunity to pause and reflect.

- What is working for you in your life now from a personal and professional perspective?
- What would you like to create in your new life abroad from a personal and professional perspective?

When we talk about thriving, we are talking about an approach to the impact of change, transition and adjustment. This approach is positive, proactive and purposeful, and it relates to the personal growth, learning and development that can result from the experience. The approach is represented by what we have named the Four Ps. Keep the Four Ps in mind as you work through the preparation and transition process. They are the basis of a robust mindset that will help you to build resilience that will support you through the adjustment process.

The Four Ps

- Positivity
- Be proactive
- Purpose
- Personal development

Our approach to Thriving Abroad comes from the fields of transition management and positive psychology.

Positivity

When we talk about being positive we aren't talking about blindly applying a positive mental attitude and seeing the good in everything. We know that there are times when things are just plain bad. Some negative reactions and thought processes are only human.

However, research by Barbara Fredrickson has shown that it is possible to notice and enjoy more positive feelings, emotions and experiences than negative. Positivity opens up our hearts and minds and makes us more receptive and creative. This in turn enables us to 'discover and build new skills, new ties, new knowledge and new ways of being'.[10]

We love this quote; it describes the benefits of positivity and also, in a nutshell, captures what we hope your experience of international mobility will give you. A mindset of positivity can only be helpful in building a new life in a new environment.

Proactive

It is easy to live a reactive life. Many expats live this way.

- 'We're only here because the company sent us. We had no choice.'
- 'We will go wherever the company chooses to send us next. We have no choice or influence.'
- 'I'm only here because my partner's job brought us here. I'd rather be anywhere else in the world.'

Phrasing decisions in this way is negative and disempowering. The reality is, in every decision we have a choice; to accept personal responsibility and ownership for the decision, embrace it and work positively and proactively to make it work as best we can.

Being proactive is about recognizing our personal power and responsibility to take charge of our own destiny. There will be many choices to make as you relocate abroad. Being proactive in making those choices and owning the outcomes will empower you through the process.

Purpose

Viktor Frankl said that 'ever more people today have the means to live, but no meaning to live for'.[11] We are all more motivated and energized when working towards something that we believe in and value.

Understanding what it is about your life that gives you a sense of purpose and meaning is an important element in developing your understanding of your personal motivation.

What is it that motivates you to want to relocate internationally?

What energizes and excites you about the possibility? Is it the thought of getting to know a different part of the world, its people, culture? Perhaps the role that you are being asked to undertake holds purpose and meaning for you? If you have children, do you see living abroad as a developmental opportunity for them? As the expat partner, are you excited by the opportunity to re-establish your career abroad, take a career break or rethink and reinvent your career?

Understanding what gives this experience purpose and meaning will give you a sense of direction, a reason why for making a life-changing decision and working through the change process successfully. It will also mean that you engage at a higher level with the experience.

Personal development

In her book *Mindset: How You Can Fulfil Your Potential*, Carol Dweck introduced us to two types of mindsets: fixed and growth.[12]

People with fixed mindsets believe that their basic qualities, such as intelligence and talent, are simply fixed traits. They focus their time on documenting their intelligence rather than developing it.

People with growth mindsets believe the opposite – that their basic abilities can be developed through dedication and hard work. Intelligence and talent are the starting points, the raw ingredients. People with growth mindsets develop a love of learning and resilience, which is valuable for accomplishment.

Can you guess which is more of an asset in the international setting?

Employing a growth mindset means recognizing the developmental opportunity of the relocation experience. You will constantly be faced with new and challenging situations, from learning a new language and cultural cues to practical work and social challenges.

At times where you're stretched and feeling that you're failing, a fixed mindset will cause you to turn away from the learning and developmental opportunity, to judge yourself as a failure or the people or situation you are interacting with as wrong. A growth mindset will encourage you to become curious, to step beyond your comfort zone and learn from the experience. It will require grit and determination but ultimately will result in personal development, resilience and resourcefulness. Learning and developing through the relocation experience will also give you a sense of accomplishment, which is rewarding.

 Reflection time 1.1

In what ways do the Four Ps feature in your life currently?

How will they help you to create a successful life abroad?

Summary

❑ What will make this experience a success for you?

❑ Everyone has a different take on what success means. Take time now to think about why you want to relocate abroad and what you want to achieve and learn from the process.

❑ Create a plan early in the relocation process so that you're ready to build your success from the moment you arrive abroad.

❑ When thinking about what success means to you, think about it from three perspectives: professional, personal and family.

❑ As an assignee, it is important to understand what will represent success from the organization's perspective.

❑ Remember that there will be a number of interested stakeholders from your organization. They may value and represent your contribution in different ways.

❑ Understand how your value will be measured so that you know how to demonstrate your value. We talk more about this in Chapter Nine.

❑ Consider how the four Ps: Positivity, Proactive, Purpose and Personal development show up in your life, now and in the future.

CHAPTER TWO

Opportunity

'Luck is what happens when preparation
meets opportunity.'
Seneca

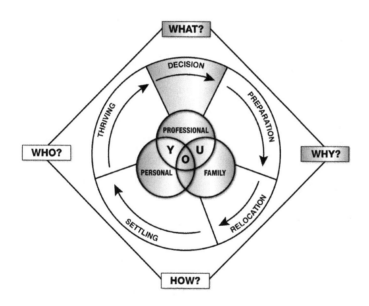

Rich and Angela

Angela sat in her best friend's house talking about the decision to accept the international assignment and move to the UK. Her friend was not impressed. She didn't get it. Didn't they have everything they wanted at home – good jobs, a lovely house carefully renovated to their liking, fantastic friends and family close by? Why would she want to leave all of that? Wouldn't she miss her work?

Now three years on, Angela is grateful to her friend for that conversation. It had been a tough and emotional one in which there were convincing arguments both ways. She had left with a sense of disquiet and determined that she and Rich needed to do some more thorough research. Were they doing the right thing? When Rich first came home with the suggestion, her initial reaction to the opportunity had not been positive. Rich had taken the lead, making a powerful argument in his eyes for going, and yet she had not been convinced. It had felt as though he was making the decision on her behalf. Rich honestly seemed to think there would be no downside. Inspired by her tough conversation with her friend Angela had insisted she and Rich consider fully all the pros and cons. Rich finally accepted that she needed some space and time to think it all through, to identify the positive aspects of the opportunity for herself; after all it had to be a joint decision. Surprisingly for Angela, as she worked through the comparison process, she saw more opportunities. Despite her friend's warnings the idea began to grow on her, and finally she caught some of Rich's enthusiasm – it was an exciting opportunity and it wasn't as though it would be forever. While they were young, why not live life differently and experience new things?

Introduction

Like many millennials, Rich saw international experience as important for him from a career development perspective. Seventy-one per cent of millennials say they expect and would like to have an overseas assignment opportunity.[13] Mobility opportunities are increasingly recognized as a way to attract, retain, develop and engage key talent.

Many organizations also recognize the value of international experience as a prerequisite for leadership roles, and global talent management is becoming a hot topic as organizations work to meet international resourcing demands.

Exciting times. Who wouldn't want to move abroad? In the popular press, expat life is portrayed as a life of privilege, adventure and opportunity.

Mention a relocation possibility to friends and colleagues and they will likely tell you how lucky you are.

We suspect that luck alone doesn't have much to do with it. The lived experience of international relocation, while fun, sometimes privileged, is often hard work – your luck or good fortune will be well earned.

Preparation will be key; the quote from Seneca above is spot on, and preparation is what much of this book is all about.

Where does this chapter fit in? Imagine you are painting a landscape. First you create the background to give the painting context. This chapter is all about understanding the context of international mobility from the perspective of opportunity and benefit. In Chapter One we talked about success and what that might look like for you from personal, professional and family perspectives. This chapter gives you the detail to help you better define what success may mean for you.

Understanding the opportunities and benefits (this chapter) and the challenges (Chapter Three) is all part of preparing to make an informed decision and working intentionally to create a thriving life abroad. Being proactive in your research and preparation for your relocation opportunity means that you will lay solid foundations for your new life abroad.

If you are considering relocating abroad to gain international experience, then you will want to know how these opportunities arise and the kinds of role that organizations look to fill.

This chapter begins with an overview of the opportunity presented by international mobility. It is useful to understand the different ways in which international experience can be attained, recognizing that it's not always necessary to relocate abroad to gain that experience. We then talk about how organizations resource their global talent and for what purpose. We finish the chapter with a look at the personal and professional benefits that come from international mobility.

Global mobility, then and now

Early expats were true adventurers and pioneers. Some were part of a colonial model of both government and trade. While their living conditions were very different from those at home, they often had high status and privilege. Others were missionaries, living lives more integrated with the local community. Adventurous wives (because then it was nearly always wives) often played an expected and acknowledged role in supporting their husbands' vocations and careers.

In the 20th century, as it became more common for people to move internationally, the model evolved but remained rooted in the old tradition, which still exists in many organizations today:

1. A role becomes available overseas.
2. An employee is offered the role either because they have expressed an interest in international opportunities OR because they have the perceived skills to perform the role.
3. A quick decision is required as there is an urgent need for someone to take the position.
4. There is an underlying assumption that the partners don't work *or* an expectation that they will compromise their careers to become *trailing spouses* and take up supporting roles.

Responding to pressure from the organization, families make quick decisions based on assumptions and with less conscious planning than one would expect. In a small survey of 153 expats, 12% of respondents were given less than one week to make a decision and 41% between one week and a month to decide.[14]

What does it mean to be globally mobile in the 21st century?

This is the 21st century, and the model described above is being challenged by a range of factors. Here, we discuss five of the most influential.

1. The ever more global world

Global mobility is expected to increase over the coming decade. Seventy-five per cent of companies believe that international assignment volumes will increase or remain the same.[15]

Organizations are introducing different ways in which international business objectives can be achieved, in addition to the traditional form of long-term assignment. In a survey conducted by PricewaterhouseCoopers (PwC), international assignees on assignment represented 1.6% of the workforce compared to 12.2% of employees who worked overseas each year.[16]

This is not to say that long-term assignments are a dying breed. Over 80% of organizations say that they still see a future for and benefit from long-term assignments.[17] However, long-term assignments represent only one way of responding to international resourcing demands and developing the appropriate international skills required for the global leadership challenges of business today.

As you consider your career and desire for international experience, take time to place it within the context of the opportunity for international mobility as outlined in the table below.

Type of international mobility	Characteristics
Long-term international assignments of two to five years	Assignee, partner and family relocate. There is a transition to an international contract of employment. Benefits are provided to support the relocation process.
Short-term international assignments of three months to one year	The employee is typically unaccompanied, although partners and families may sometimes join depending on circumstances. The benefits offered are generally not as generous as those in long-term assignments.
Commuter assignments of three to six months	The employee is away from home from Monday to Friday and returns for the weekend. The benefit is that the family does not have to relocate as well.
	Challenges include: • taxation (where is the employee judged to be employed?); • compliance (entry and work visas); • impact on family of an absentee partner; and • stress of regular long-haul flights.
Fly in, fly out	After a designated work period in one country, the employee flies home to rest before repeating. Often used in the oil, gas and engineering sectors. See Commuter assignments for benefits and challenges.
International business traveller	The employee remains in the home country and travels for business meetings. See Commuter assignments for benefits and challenges.

Split family assignments	The whole family moves to one location (Dubai, for example) and the employee commutes to work in another location (such as Iraq) Sunday through to Thursday.
	This may occur due to challenges regarding education for children and work opportunities for partners, or due to safety and security concerns.
	The benefit is that the possible negative implications of a hardship posting are avoided.
	The challenges include: • impact on family of an absentee partner; • loneliness for partner and family in a new and unfamiliar environment; and • stress of regular travel for employee.
One-way permanent moves	The employee and family are moved to a new location with the intention of remaining there indefinitely. These are often driven by the employee although may be the result of a head office relocation with employees offered the choice of moving or leaving the company.

N.B. You may have noticed a cap between 12 and 24 months. The way in which assignments of this duration are treated will depend on whether they are considered long short-term assignments or short long-term assignments. Different organizations will have different practices.

2. The demand for global talent

In response to demographic changes and the anticipated 'war for global talent',[18] organizations are recognizing the need for more focused global talent management programmes. Michael White, chairman, president and CEO of The DirecTV Group Inc., in a PwC report, highlighted the scale of the future talent challenge in the US, saying:

'There are 80 million baby boomers (US) who are going to retire over the next five to seven years, and they're going to be replaced by 40 million generation Xers. That's two to one, so you'd better be developing your next generation now if you're going to be ready for that transition.'[19]

The expectation is that it will become more difficult for organizations to recruit and retain talent, meaning that they must become more strategic in their talent management processes.

As a result, some organizations are more consciously investing in people, with specific intentions and career trajectories for targeted people. This rigorous approach to managing assignments is facilitated by the emergence of 'big data' – data that enables HR professionals to support this strategic, ROI-based approach. Though discussed frequently, the approach is still in its infancy.

3. The development of more complex geographical relocation flows

The relocation flows of international mobility are becoming more complex with the growth of the BRIC countries (Brazil, Russia, India and China) and other developing countries. With this expansion comes the need for internationally mobile employees.

In the past, the flow was generally from the head office country to the subsidiary. Senior management was sent to install management practices and processes and to convey the organizational culture. Today the assignment purpose and locational opportunities are much wider. Flow is multidirectional, multifunctional and multilevel in terms of seniority of the assignees, ranging from interns and graduates through to senior leaders.

The relocation experience can differ enormously depending on the geographical location. Developing countries such as China and India can offer great opportunities to assignees that have the appetite for adventure and a sense of engagement with their organization's goals for those regions of the world. However, it can be a step too far for some people, or their partners and families.

One of the challenges that organizations currently face is that potential assignees are more motivated to relocate to developed countries such as the UK, USA and Australia than they are the developing countries. Conversely, organizations want people to go to emerging markets.[20]

If you are considering the international assignment opportunity from a general interest perspective, take time now to think about where in the world you and your partner/family would be prepared to relocate. If you have been offered an assignment opportunity in a specific location, research the opportunities and challenges that you might face in moving there. Consider it not only from the work role perspective but also in terms of general quality of life, safety, security, education and professional opportunities for your partner, where that is relevant.

4. The challenge of dual career expatriates

Dual career couples are those where both partners are earning an income and are each committed to their respective careers. Increasingly, families rely on dual incomes for their financial welfare. This can mean that prospective assignees are forced to turn down assignments to avoid the negative career impact for their partners, or may never enter into the international mobility arena in the first place. This has an impact on the way in which organizations are able to resource international positions.

However, many partners do choose to embark on international relocation, recognizing the positive experiences and opportunities that can arise. Technology gives partners many more options to maintain, build or reinvent a career while living overseas. Organizations are becoming more aware of the value of providing support for partners and families, including the family in pre-assignment processes, and providing spousal and child-related benefits.

5. Organizational support for international mobility

There was a time when international mobility was seen by assignees as an opportunity to save for their future. Organizations used financial incentives to persuade senior managers to take on responsibilities abroad. Today, cost constraints leading to lower budgets, less perceived hardship and the pervasiveness of international assignments mean that being an expat is no longer as financially lucrative. In general, companies are under more pressure to keep costs down, with most companies reporting an effort to reduce assignment costs.

The global mobility opportunity: Who and why?

As we have just seen, the good news is that the opportunity for international exposure is much greater today than it was 30 years ago, and the range of ways in which that exposure may be experienced is broader.

Who relocates

Organizations have two routes when resourcing international positions: appointing internal candidates or recruiting externally.

The internal opportunity

Generally, internal candidates are initially preferred as they have a known track record and are more embedded in the organization – they understand its goals, culture and values and established networks. Often assignees are selected based on past performance and/or personal connections within the organization. But as in the investment world, past performance is no guide to future return, and good performance abroad often requires cross-cultural communication and global leadership skills. Prior exposure to multicultural teamwork, languages and cultures, and a disposition for acquiring these skills and competencies, is increasingly sought for many international managerial and leadership roles.

The use of inpatriates, or foreign local hires, is becoming more prevalent in big global organizations as they move people from their subsidiaries or other group companies to take on roles in the home country.

The external opportunity

Around 40% of organizations believe they have insufficient internal talent to meet their international resourcing needs. This presents a significant challenge.[21]

There is also debate about whether bringing in a foreigner to perform a leadership role is always the best strategy. It takes time for the assignee to integrate, and there is always the chance that they will be seen as the 'foreigner in charge'[22] rather than part of the home management team.

One solution is to recruit locally, looking for host country nationals who have the appropriate skills and talents. This approach is cost saving. However, finding the right talent can prove challenging, particularly in developing countries where the appropriate managerial or technical skills may not exist.

An alternative is to recruit from a growing population of mobile or global employees – global careerists or self-initiated expats. These are people who are developing their own international careers independently of any one organization's support. They may be home country nationals already residing in the country where the vacancy exists, or third country nationals, who live inside or outside the country in question but who are prepared to relocate for the job opportunity.[23]

There is a cost advantage in selecting these people as well, as relocation costs are minimized. The risk is they are not known to the organization or embedded in the same way as longer-term employees; their loyalty may not be assured. On the plus side, though, due to their independent status they may be more committed to making a positive impact in order to influence their longer-term future in the organization or their reputation and standing in the wider market should they choose to move on.

Understanding why assignment opportunities arise

Ideally, the assignment needs to generate a win-win for the assignee, partner, family *and* organization. This is a big ask, which starts at the preparation and planning stage. The opportunity must have a clear purpose and value for all parties.

It can be difficult to ensure that this happens for a number of reasons. There might be a number of interested parties all with differing goals and perspectives; an assignment opportunity might arise in response to an urgent business need, meaning there is insufficient time to analyse the need from a strategic perspective or assure a good fit between role and assignee; goals and objectives might not be well defined, meaning assignment outcomes are difficult to measure.

Understanding the purpose of international assignments

Deloitte proposes two important dimensions to consider when thinking about the attractiveness of international assignments from the organizational perspective.[24]

- The **business need/value** of an assignment, which runs from low to high business value.
- The **developmental value** of an assignment to the assignee, which runs from low to high developmental value.

In applying these two dimensions, businesses and assignees can analyse the related value of different assignment opportunities.

Consider the following.

Low business value and low developmental value. These jobs need filling but not necessarily by high-cost assignees. Businesses will seek to fill these roles locally, or with volunteers or perhaps interns.

Low business value and high developmental value. One of the more frequently cited reasons for international assignment in global mobility surveys is the developmental nature of the international role. Graduate rotational assignments or leadership development roles fall into this category. Initially they may offer little direct business value, but the investment in employee development is expected to pay off in the long term as newly developed skills and knowledge are utilized in future roles.

High business value and low developmental value. A popular purpose for international assignment is to resolve a specific business need using existing management or technical skills. There is perhaps little job-related technical skill and knowledge development that results for the assignee, but there will be skill development that relates to the expat and international experience.

High business value and high developmental value. These jobs involve developing and transferring highly skilled employees – perhaps existing or potential business leaders who have been identified as superstars and for whom developing global mindset and leadership skills is important.

Understanding where your potential or actual role may sit within these four categories will help you to judge the purpose and value of your role to your organization.

What does this mean for you?

As the assignee:

- Consider the kind of role that appeals. What is its purpose? How does it fit your career aspirations, and how can you influence it? Investigate whether your organization has an assignment talent pool. If so, how can you become a part of that pool?
- If you're working for an organization with a home base elsewhere, would you relocate to the headquarters as an inpatriate? What opportunities and roles are available for this in your organization?
- If you think that your current organization is unlikely to have appropriate opportunities for you, where else could you look? Where in the world would you relocate to? What roles are you qualified to undertake? How do you feel about taking the initiative and developing your own career as a global careerist?

As the partner:

- If you want to continue your current career abroad, investigate the opportunities available in appropriate businesses in your destination countries. Some companies are prepared to consider dual assignments, where roles are found for both assignee and partner. Or they may be members of the International Dual Career Network, which aims to provide access to a turnkey pool of international talent, thereby facilitating job searches for the partners of international assignees.
- Check whether obtaining a work visa is possible and whether your professional qualifications will be recognized.
- If you think you'll be unable to work in your current role, or wish to develop your career in a new direction, start to think about other possibilities.

Considering these issues proactively enables you to make the most of opportunities as they arise. You'll know that your decisions are based on a sound understanding of what you want to gain from the international experience from a professional perspective.

 Reflection time 2.0

What are the international opportunities that may arise for you?

How can you influence those opportunities positively?

Benefits of international mobility

Understanding the motivation behind accepting an international assignment is important for both the assignee and partner.

Think about the benefits from the three perspectives of the Venn diagram YOU, which is at the centre of the Framework for Thriving Abroad.

Professional benefits

What will international relocation do for you professionally? In this section, we talk about the benefits in terms of career and professional development, skills and knowledge development, network development and finances.

Career and professional development

For the assignee, part of the motivation for relocating internationally is the positive impact the experience will have on their future career development. Seventy-seven per cent of respondents to the Brookfield Global Relocation Trends Survey, Mindful Mobility[25] believed that international experience had real value in terms of acquiring specialized knowledge and leadership skills, giving employees a clear advantage over peers with no international experience.

For the partner, the benefit from a career perspective may not be so clear. Where original careers can be pursued abroad, the benefits can be equal to those of the assignee.

Even where original careers cannot be pursued, there can still be opportunity for personal and professional development. Partners say that international relocation gives them:

- the opportunity to pursue their careers abroad – while challenging to secure a role abroad, it can be extremely rewarding;
- the space and time to review their career trajectory and create change where it is desired, resulting in complete career reinvention;
- the opportunity to retrain, or to engage in further study; and
- the opportunity for a career break and to spend time with their children and focus on family.

For those partners who are career driven, it can be challenging to face a career void. But those who embrace the challenge often have exciting professional and personal outcomes to share. Their international experience is often instrumental in creating positive professional change and development.

Sometimes the opportunities may not be quite what we expected but truly life enhancing nonetheless. Chantal Duke, a global mobility specialist, relocated numerous times with her partner, a US diplomat. Her approach was to get involved, immerse herself in the local culture and language, and this led her career in diverse directions. An interest in food led Chantal to initiate a social cooking group in Ethiopia, and this gave her the skills to run a restaurant when her family was reassigned to Chad. In her next move, Chantal taught languages in a local school, where she learned a lot about planning and different educational systems which, she believes, contributed to her current position in an international school in the US. She says:

'I've been very, very lucky, I think, in every place I moved to as an adult to find unusual opportunities by being open to what was out there. Sometimes I could not work in the local markets because of visa restrictions, so I would stay active by creating social groups and volunteering, with my main focus on supporting hospitals, schools and orphanages. I also worked with local artists in Chile, Ethiopia, Chad and Mexico and learned from their techniques for my own art work. That has allowed me to develop an understanding of local traditions, build great friendships and acquire unique skills of resilience and adaptation to changes. So, being culturally very active in local communities and being open to unexpected professional opportunities helped me to gain great experience and skills, in spite of the challenges expatriates face at every move.'

Skills and knowledge development

'International living is not only relocating, it is life learning.'[26]

The true developmental value of international relocation comes from integrating with other cultures and developing cultural agility and a global mindset. In the workplace this is particularly important, as the ability to integrate well leads to the development of trust and influence, which in turn impacts role performance.

You will not develop a global mindset by relocating internationally and operating within your own cultural framework and norms. Relocation needs to be a conscious process based on self-awareness, personal reflection and additional support in terms of training and coaching. This does not always happen as Paula Caligiuri explains here:

'In today's corporate halls, business trips and international assignments accumulate like knowledge chips. Although international business travel and international assignments can be highly developmental, the talent management metric for judging cultural agility should not be frequency or duration of trips to a foreign country.'[27]

However, when you do step out and work to understand the local culture, to interact and live within it, the acquisition of valued and relevant skills is your reward. You develop both hard and soft skills.

Hard skills include things like proficiency in a foreign language and role-related technical skills and knowledge. The extent to which the assignment is beneficial in respect to hard skills will depend on the roles in which you work, their remit and scope.

Soft skills are more subjective abilities, which are more difficult to quantify but are in demand. In a Heidrick and Struggles report, Karl-Heinz Oehler says that the rarest personality traits in leaders are resilience, adaptability, intellectual agility and versatility and that:

'The biggest need now is for leaders with the ability to deal with a changing situation and not get paralyzed by it...'[28]

Here we list the skills, strengths and capabilities developed through an international relocation.

- *Adaptability/flexibility* is the ability to change, or be changed, to fit circumstances.
- *Resilience* is the ability to cope with stress and calamity. Resilient people utilize their skills and strengths to cope with and recover from problems and challenges.
- *Personal confidence* is the confidence that comes from stepping out of your comfort zone and succeeding.
- *Cultural and intellectual agility* is 'the mega-competency that enables professionals to perform successfully in cross-cultural situations.'[28]

- *Global mindset* is 'a set of attributes and characteristics that help global leaders better influence individuals, groups, and organisations unlike themselves.'[29]

  Mansour Javidan, Director of the Najafi Global Mindset Institute, says global mindset is important for 21st century leadership, which requires the ability to think and make decisions globally and understand global challenges and opportunities.

- *Social interaction skills* are the skills needed to adapt and integrate into a new social structure.
- *Creativity* is the ability to develop innovative solutions to challenges.
- *Organizational skills* are those that involve planning (coordinating the relocation experience requires sound organizational skills).
- *Independence and self-sufficiency* involve moving away from your normal support structures and coping with everyday challenges with your partner/family.
- *Leadership capabilities* draw on many of the skills listed above.

Whether you are living abroad or interacting culturally through business trips or international teams, these skills will be necessary and invaluable.

Network development

One of the benefits of international relocation from both a personal and professional perspective is the opportunity to expand your network of connections. The international environment is a hugely supportive one. All expats appreciate the value of support when living far away from friends and family and are usually prepared to offer a helping hand. You will develop a network over time of international and host national connections – this resource is valuable and life enhancing. Interacting with a wide-based network will also help you develop the global mindset and leadership skills discussed above.

Financial benefits

In a Cartus survey, 34% of respondents said that money was important in influencing assignees' decisions to relocate,[30] and anecdotally, expatriates tell us that the financial benefits of international mobility do explain in part their motivation. When thinking about the financial benefits, it is important to set them within the context of the entire package of benefits and the impact of those benefits on your partner and family. We talk more about this in the next two chapters.

Personal benefits

It is rare to meet an expat who doesn't think that their time abroad has been invaluable in terms of experiences and, for some, adventure. We let the voices of expats explain why:[31]

'Exploring new locations and cultures, meeting new people, making new contacts, improving my language skills, establishing new routines and traditions.'

'Getting to know the people in the local environment, their values, and learning to understand their way of living.'

'Learning about the world. Living abroad has been such an eye-opening experience, I am forever grateful for the opportunity and for the lessons I'm learning.'

Volunteering is a way to contribute while abroad, and for the partner who is unable to work, it's often a valuable route to finding meaning and purpose in the relocation experience.

It is important as the assignee not to lose sight of this potential benefit, and to ensure that time for personal interests and hobbies is built into the equation as well.

Family benefits (with or without children)

There are many benefits of international relocation from the family perspective.

The relationship between partners can be strengthened

It is generally acknowledged that where the relationship was strong at the outset, an expat experience may strengthen it further, provided that communication pathways are kept open and the basis of trust in the relationship is not challenged.

The partner has space and time to devote to the family unit

In our Career Choice and the Accompanying Partner survey, 22% of participants said that they were not interested in working while abroad. They pointed to the benefits of staying home and caring for their families and/or developing their own activities, stating they were able to participate more in school and voluntary events. This comment illustrates this perspective: 'Be aware that employment is not the only answer to finding self. We have new/other opportunities to discover who we are and "measure worth"!'[32]

Families can become closer

Relocating as a family and with children involves challenges, and we discuss these in Chapter Four. Despite the challenges, many families recognize that the experience ultimately brings them closer as a family unit.

One advantage is that parents develop strong relationships with their children and vice versa. Seeing each other struggle at different times with the process of change and supporting each other through the emotional fallout creates stronger ties, understanding, and relationships.

Benefits for children

Children benefit from international relocation for many reasons.

1. *They build resilience.* While relocating can be tough for children, as they must say goodbye to homes, friends and family, the upside is that they develop their internal emotional resources to navigate the challenges of moving.
2. *They learn to be adaptable.* They learn to become comfortable with change and adapt their way of being to the new surroundings and circumstances.
3. *They develop a broad view of the world.* Living in different countries, children develop their cultural understanding and cross-cultural communication skills, learning to see life from different perspectives.
4. *They develop personal confidence.* 'New' no longer fazes them, and they develop confidence to deal with new situations.
5. *They don't see differences.* Many expat children attend international schools where there are broad representations of different nationalities. This means that everyone is different so no one is different. Children who have lived international lives tend to look for the things that give them common bonds and ignore the differences.
6. *They learn new languages.* Perhaps they even become bilingual or trilingual. This comes with great benefits, as Rita Rosenback outlines in her book *Bringing Up A Bilingual Child*:[33]
   - the ability to communicate more widely;
   - the ability to communicate consciously and sensitively, due to their understanding of the differences between languages;
   - increased cultural understanding;

- 'improved memory (research has shown that bilingual people have, on average, a better memory than monolinguals)';
- 'increased creativity (in tests, bilingual children have shown more creative thinking than monolinguals)';
- ease in learning additional languages; and
- better employment prospects, due to their ability to communicate with a wider number of contacts.

 Reflection time 2.1

What are the opportunities and benefits of international mobility that most appeal to you?

Summary

❑ There are a variety of ways in which international exposure can be obtained and international experience built.
   - Long-term assignments, two to five years
   - Short-term assignments, usually between nine and twelve months
   - Commuter assignments
   - Rotational assignments
   - Fly in, fly out assignments
   - International business traveller assignments
   - Split family assignments
   - Virtual assignments
   - One-way permanent moves

❑ It is important to gain clarity over your career and life aspirations, but keep an open mind and be 'luck ready'.[34]

❑ Organizations recruit for international positions internally and externally. Do you want to be an organizational assignee or an independent global careerist?

❑ The decision to relocate, from both the individual and the organizational perspective, needs to be based on clarity of purpose and value for *both* the organization and the assignee, partner and family.

❑ It is important for the assignee to have clarity over the purpose of the position/role in terms of its value to the organization and its developmental value.

❑ Understand and investigate the benefits of relocation to you and your family. Think about the benefits in terms of:

- Career development
- Developing skills and knowledge
- Expanding personal and professional networks
- Financial benefits
- Lifestyle, life experiences and adventures
- Benefits to you and your partner and/or family
- Benefits to your children

CHAPTER THREE

Challenges

. . . .

'Forewarned, forearmed; to be prepared is
half the victory.'
Miguel de Cervantes

. . . .

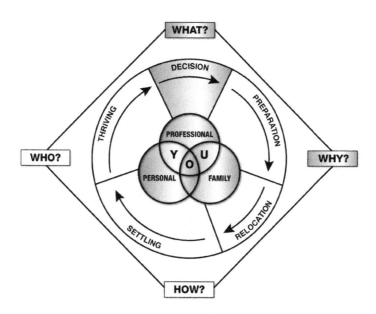

Jenny and Paul

Jenny called Paul and asked him to have dinner with a couple who were in Shanghai on a look-see visit. They were considering a position with one of the companies she partnered with. The wife, Jean, wanted to speak to Paul as she was giving up her job back home to move. She was keen to find something new but also wanted to know about the potential challenges and pitfalls, how to be best prepared. Jenny had told her about Paul's challenges and that he was now studying for an MBA. It couldn't do any harm, he supposed, to tell her about their experience. It would help this couple avoid making the same mistakes and hopefully settle a little more quickly than he and Jenny had. He was enjoying the experience now, but boy had it been hard in those early weeks and months. Paul had found leaving his career behind and the consequential loss of income more challenging than he had imagined. Being financially dependent on Jenny had felt strange, and managing on only Jenny's income had been difficult in those early, expensive settling-in months. Then there were the children. Watching the kids' tentative first days and weeks at school had been tough – it was a much bigger school than the little primary they had attended back home. They had been intimidated by the hustle, the noise. They'd even cried some days at the school gate, and that made him feel guilty. Had he and Jenny been selfish to uproot them from all they knew and loved back home? He had also felt quite alone in those early weeks. Jenny had been extremely busy settling into her new job with responsibilities that were wider ranging that she had expected. He wondered whether she had ever seen a full job description; he thought not. She was coping OK now, but it had been tough to see her as stressed as she was at the start. He had worried about her. This new couple had two children in their early teens, and Paul wondered how they felt about moving. Good that Jean was thinking about finding work now, rather than after arriving. He would suggest she request support for her job search process – support he hadn't had. It would be tough, but he knew expat partners who had found work. You just needed to hang in there and stick with it. Reflecting back, Paul wished he'd had someone to help show him the ropes, to highlight the potential pitfalls before they made their move.

Introduction

In Chapter Two, we talked about the benefits and opportunities of a global lifestyle. Here, we turn the table to highlight the potential challenges and hotspots of international relocation.

When we think back on our personal deliberations about relocation, we recognize that we sugar-coated the potential experience in our minds perhaps just a little!

And it turns out that this is quite a natural human tendency.

We all have a natural 'optimism bias'; we often believe the future will be better than the past and present.[35] This means that when thinking about the future we can make overly optimistic assumptions that can turn to disappointment when reality does not match those expectations. Sometimes this can be quite disastrous.

The problem with sugar-coating is that it can lead to unrealistic expectations, which may affect our adjustment process, often when we are feeling most vulnerable.

It is worth bearing this tendency in mind as you consider relocating. This is not to put you off, but to help you avoid making a decision based upon overly positive assumptions.

As you read this chapter, keep your optimism bias in check and look for a balance between the optimistic ideal and realistic expectations. There is evidence to suggest that where expectations are realistic, the adjustment process is smoother.[36]

A few words about expatriate adjustment

Relocating internationally changes everything. With change comes adjustment, which is rarely a linear process. You may have heard of the concept of culture shock. This is an emotional or psychological reaction that occurs when people are subjected to an unfamiliar culture characterized by different traditions, behaviours, attitudes and beliefs.

The degree to which culture shock is experienced will differ from person to person and is related to the adjustment you need to make to the change in your work, general and social (interactional) environments. You will find yourself adjusting:

- to the new work role, culture and environment;
- to the general living environment and culture and the language of your day-to-day interactions; and
- to the changing nature of your relationships back home and to new friendships and support networks abroad.[37]

An experience of contrasts

Change will occur in every area of your life, as well as your family's and will have an emotional, psychological and behavioural impact. Reactions may be both positive and negative; for example, you may feel sad to leave loved ones behind but excited and inspired by the prospect of new beginnings. You may find that you behave positively and enthusiastically some days and then fall into a sense of overwhelm and frustration on others. International relocation is a blend of experiences: intense, fun, challenging, rewarding, scary and exciting.

We can't erase these contrasts for you, but we can help you to research, plan and set realistic expectations for your new life abroad. This way there will be fewer unwelcome surprises along the way.

In deciding to accept an international assignment you are taking a risk from a career, family and financial perspective. In today's corporate environment nobody can make promises about the future. This means it's important to think the decision through carefully and check that you are comfortable with the potential uncertainty. Basing your decision on a sound appreciation of the challenges can help to reduce any associated risks.

Relocation hotspots

In this chapter, we focus on the most common hotspots, which are broken down into four areas as shown in the diagram below.

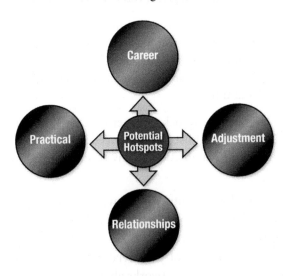

Relocation Hotspots

We highlight the challenges and provide 'thinking points' for consideration. The points discussed in this chapter are not deal-breakers. We point them out to help you make an informed decision. Understanding both the opportunities and the challenges means you will be able to create appropriate strategies to eliminate or minimize any negative effects. We suggest creating a list of the pros and cons of international relocation. This chapter provides many of the cons (Chapter Two focuses on the pros).

Career challenges

Assignee career-related challenges

Jenny found the work transition stressful, and this is not unusual. The challenge of adjusting to a new role back home can be daunting; add in the additional challenges of moving your entire life to a new location and adjusting to a new culture and perhaps language and you can see why it might be one of life's more stressful events. The following issues can create career challenges.

The role

- Blinded by the great opportunity of living and working abroad, like Jenny, the assignee may not research the scale and scope of the role they are being asked to perform, resulting in surprise and potential overwhelm.
- The work role may be too great a stretch given the assignee's skills and knowledge, or the cultural work environment may call on understanding, skills or knowledge that the assignee does not possess.
- The role may be overblown to attract the assignee, leading to disappointment when the reality hits home.
- The commitment required in terms of hours worked, daily commutes and international travel may be greater than expected.
- The work and the living environment may be unpleasant and disappointing.
- The role may be fine, but not all assignments end in promotion and positive next steps.

The contractual agreement

Many of the points above and many of the points to be discussed will be covered in the contract of employment. Mistakes are made when:

- the assignee is not clear about what needs to be included in the assignment package;

- the contract of employment is not carefully reviewed by the assignee and partner prior to signing; and
- the contract of employment is not signed prior to departure (if something goes wrong, there is no supporting legal document).

THINKING POINTS:

- Ensure that you have clarity about the job role you are being asked to perform. Meet with relevant managers to discuss your role and expected outcomes/targets, pay and bonuses.
- Understand what standard support your organization is generally prepared to provide and where additional benefits may be negotiated in individual circumstances (see Chapter Four for more details).
- Organize a familiarization visit for you and your partner prior to agreeing to the assignment, if possible.
- Consider your skill set and strengths. Is there a good fit with the role requirements? Where are the gaps? What training and support should be provided to help with these gaps? For example, cross-cultural understanding, language acquisition or executive coaching support?
- Think about the potential for stress and how you have handled it in the past. Consider the strategies that have worked for you before.
- Discus these work-related hotspots with your partner so that you are both aware of the challenges and can work together to eliminate the risks or develop strategies to cope.
- Talk to HR about the future trajectory of your career post international assignment (it is never too early to start this conversation).
- Find a mentor to help you manage your career forward. Bear in mind that the best person to speak to about your future career may not be your boss. As Kristen, international assignee and Head of HR for a large multinational company, says:

'I recommend to international assignees you need to talk to the Regional or Global HR person who is masterminding your move and understand under what premise they're justifying it. Are they justifying it as a skills transfer? That's a completely different scenario than if they're justifying it because they are developing you for bigger roles. I'd recommend people having that sponsorship, preferably a few levels up. Your boss holding a spot for you to come home too is not realistic at all especially

> as you grow and change and want something bigger over time which most of us do.'

- Consider your attitude to living with uncertainty, as this is a feature, perhaps even a trade-off, of expat life. How important is stability to you?

We provide more specific guidance about the contract and look-see visits in the research section of Chapter Four.

Partner career-related challenges

Many expat partners don't work while they live abroad; for some, this may not be by choice. While there are opportunities to build new careers, there are also many obstacles that prevent partners from working, such as inability to obtain a work visa, non-recognition of qualifications, language and cultural challenges, the need for flexibility to be able to look after children, and difficulty in securing short-term employment.

The truth is, it is often very difficult, though not impossible, to replicate home careers abroad.

In an interview, Kristen, international assignee and Head of HR for a large multi-national company, made the following observation:

> 'It can be challenging to mix two alpha careers. One of the things I see often is that the partner assumes that once they get settled they're just going to pick up where they left off and be super marketable in the host country. I have literally yet to see that happen and so I usually try to set low expectations, because it's really, really hard. There are the language challenges, and then the fact that assignments are generally short term and employers are loathe to hire with the knowledge that people will be moving on. I know no one wants to talk about that but that's the reality. The moment that you make a decision that someone's going to move for their career that means the other person puts themselves in a secondary position career wise. I'm not saying you can't then decide to move for the partner's career later.'

Food for thought indeed. We do know partners who have created engaging careers abroad – for example, Chantal (Chapter Two) and Jacquie (Chapter

Five). It takes a dedicated, proactive approach and an open mind. You can listen to other expat partners share their stories, tips and insights on the Thriving Abroad podcast, and Chapter Ten is devoted to the experience of expat partners and how, irrespective of gender, they can make the international experience work both personally and professionally.

A non-working partner might:

- become demoralized early in the assignment experience due to unmet career expectations (like Paul);
- feel isolated, especially if the couple have no children;
- lack a sense of purpose and meaning in their everyday life (our podcast interviews speak to exactly this point);
- suffer financial pressures that result from the loss of one income;
- become financially dependent (as Paul described, it can feel disempowering if you're used to being in charge of your personal income);
- feel that their personal identity is challenged (they are no longer partly defined by their professional work role and relationships with colleagues); and
- lose their professional confidence over time, making returning to the workforce more challenging.

One partner who accompanied her boyfriend to Asia found life challenging as she had no work permit. Though she worked hard to keep herself busy by attending social groups and volunteering in an orphanage, she found not having a purpose difficult:

'I just try to keep busy, go to the gym, attend expat events, Meetups and InterNations, but after a while… you get listless and bored. We all want to be independent and strong-minded. I'm well educated, feeling a loss of independence, and being the person who follows is tough.'

Despite the challenges, she didn't feel that she would change her decision if she had her time again.

THINKING POINTS:

- Consider your professional/career aspirations. How important is your current career to you?

- Research your legal work status in the host country. Will a work visa be readily available? If not, what is the process and who will support that process?
- Check whether professional qualifications are recognized in your target country.
- Consider how you feel about starting a career search in another country and culture.
- Consider, if your career is not transferable, how you feel about career reinvention or taking a career break.
- Research career possibilities in the new location – speak to recruitment consultants and equivalent professionals or people doing similar jobs in the host company.
- Consider how you can maintain or develop your professional skills and knowledge while you are abroad, perhaps through further study or volunteer work.
- Understand the career support provided by the assigning organization for the partner.

 Reflection time 3.0

What career/professional issues and challenges do you need to consider and research before making your decision?

What do you need to know and understand so that you can make an informed decision?

General adjustment hotspots

Mindset

Your attitude to the relocation decision and experience affects how you perceive your adjustment and settle into your new life abroad.

Mindset issues that may impact the success of an assignment, from both a personal and professional perspective, include:

- a belief that the assignment is imposed and that there is no choice. One partner shared this story:

'You know you need an open mind, otherwise you could be miserable. I know a woman who was a lawyer back home in her country. She relocated with her partner and a two year old. She is very unhappy and doesn't want to do anything. She just doesn't want to be here and this attitude has impacted on her whole approach and experience.'

- unrealistic expectations (due to lack of research);
- frustration with the assigning organization for a perceived lack of support (this can affect the assignee's and partner's engagement with the whole experience);
- a culturally superior mindset (it's never good to begin with the belief that there is nothing to learn, that how you do everything back home is the best and only way);
- fear that the culture and language will be impossible to master (meaning that you run away from opportunities to learn and integrate socially);
- a tendency for pessimism (which is ironic, given our earlier discussion of the optimism bias – but there are benefits to an optimism bias in terms of adapting to new circumstances; we like to talk in terms of realistic optimism and positivity); and
- a lack of personal agency and willingness to take responsibility for creating a successful new life abroad.

THINKING POINTS:

- Be honest about your reaction to this opportunity. Does it cause you to contract in fear, expand in enthusiasm and excitement or something in between?
- Think about your general mindset. Do you tend to run away from new experiences and learning, scared that you may fail? Or do you enjoy taking on new challenges, accepting that it's your responsibility to make it work for you? It's important to relocate with a positive, can-do attitude.
- Remember the Four Ps. Being proactive and approaching the experience with positivity will help to make the experience more enjoyable.

Partner/family adjustment

In a relocation survey, 91% of respondents said that overcoming the challenge of family adjustment was either very critical or of high importance in relation to the success of an international assignment.[38] An unhappy partner and/or family can have a serious impact on the assignee's work performance and desire to see the assignment through.

What are the typical adjustment challenges?

- Language challenges can make even the simplest of tasks difficult and time consuming, not to mention stressful.
- Like Jenny, the assignee may find adjusting to their new work role stressful from a cultural and managerial perspective. This stress may spill over to the home environment and affect relationships and stability at home.[39]
- Like Paul, the partner may miss their career and find adjusting to their new support role and financial dependence difficult.
- Stress – relocating internationally is inherently stressful:

> 'Of the 40 most stressful life events, at least half can be directly or indirectly associated with the international relocation of a family, including a change in financial status, a change or new line of work, wife starting or stopping work, and changes in residence, school and social activities.'[40]

- Children find adjusting to new schools challenging, especially where schools are not used to receiving international students.
- Missing friends and family back home, coupled with resentment at being pulled away from all that is familiar, can be a major issue, particularly for teenagers.
- It can take time to develop new friendships and social networks; in the meantime, there can be a sense of isolation, especially when the assignee is working long hours or travelling frequently.
- When things don't happen as expected, frustration and/or a sense of inadequacy can result.

THINKING POINTS:

- Recognize the scale of the change that you are undertaking. On paper, it looks as though it's just the geographical location that is changing. In reality, everything changes. This means there is always going to be some fallout and some negative implications. It won't be about just the challenges or just the opportunities. There will be a balance.
- Familiarize yourself with the transition process so that you know what to expect. Fortunately this is what this book is all about!

- Communicate honestly about how you are feeling right from the beginning. Talk about the positive, exciting aspects of relocation *and* the challenges.

Reflection time 3.1

What adjustment challenges might you experience?

What can you do in the decision-making and preparation phases to minimize their effect?

Relationship hotspots

Financial dependency

As the introductory case study to this chapter illustrated, partners who leave a career and income behind become dependent from a financial perspective on the assignee, perhaps for the first time. This can create challenging dynamics within the relationship and create sensitivities over the management of the family and household finances.

THINKING POINTS:

Think through the implications of financial dependency from a personal perspective, and then talk through them with your partner. Consider:

- how the partner feels about being financially dependent on the assignee;
- how the assignee feels about the responsibility of being the sole earner; and
- how the situation will be managed from a relational perspective. It can impact on the balance of power within a relationship unless managed in an open and mutually supportive way.

Relationship breakdown and divorce

The Brookfield Global Relocation Trends Survey 2015 found that 74% of expatriates relocate with a spouse/partner and 52% relocate with children.[41] The harsh truth is that relationships break down wherever you are in the world, and the implications of a breakdown abroad, especially where children are involved, can be catastrophic for all concerned.

It is not that divorce among the expatriate population is any more prevalent, says Yvonne McNulty, 'but… it has been found to have more serious implications and outcomes than divorce that takes place in one's home country'.[42]

What contributes to relationship breakdown while abroad?

McNulty suggests that there are two main contributing factors:

1. An important issue existed in the marriage before the couple went abroad and then continued while abroad (a mental health problem, alcoholism, domestic or psychological abuse, etc.).
2. One or both spouses are negatively influenced by the new environment to such an extent that they behave differently from how they would do back home. [43]

Lucy Greenwood, a partner at the Family Law Group, LLP, agrees and says the clients who worry her the most are those in category one, who move abroad to 'fix their relationships'.[44] Category two is obviously harder to predict.

For the dependent, non-working partner, the impact of a relationship breakdown can be considerable, as this quote demonstrates:

> 'I have been financially dependent on my husband for all of our expatriate years, and I have no idea how I am going to survive and make a living for myself from now on.'[45]

When children are involved, the situation can become even more challenging and complex from a legal perspective, particularly if one partner wants to stay abroad and the other wants to return to their home country.

THINKING POINTS:

- If you have a proposed relocation destination, investigate whether your relationship will be recognized or are even deemed legal in that location, particularly if you are cohabiting or in a same-sex marriage.
- Think carefully about your relationship. Consider whether an international relocation is appropriate if you are motivated to move in order to repair a broken relationship.
- Talk honestly and openly about the opportunity of international relocation and, importantly, discuss how long you plan to stay abroad and what will happen if it doesn't work out for one or both of you or the children.
- Consider how you will build time for you as a couple into the relocation experience. Focus on honest and open communication.

Social support networks

We are social animals, and social support and connection are our lifeblood. In the early days of an assignment, social connections help you to find your feet and acquire the basic information required to settle in.

Challenges that expats may face:

- the absence of social support in the early days (i.e., no connection or communication with people who can act as local guides and advisers);
- language challenges (which make it difficult to form new social connections);
- loneliness;
- an expectation that it will be easy;
- coming to terms with leaving behind established social networks, family and friends (this is tough for everyone but particularly children and teens); and
- for children and teenagers, developing new friendships and attachments in new schools.

THINKING POINTS:

- If you know the proposed host location, start to research the local expat groups and special interest groups now. InterNations (www.internations.org) is a worldwide organization that offers social groups in over 390 cities around the world. You can also become a member and begin to network online. It's a great place to ask questions and find out more about the host location. There are also a wealth of other forums and groups that you can join, including the Thriving Abroad Forum in the book membership area. Go to the resources section of this book for more ideas and connections.
- Ask your organization to connect you with colleagues in your host location. This seems so simple and yet so few organizations routinely do it.
- Think about how you will maintain connections with friends and relatives back home. Face Time, Facebook, Instagram and Skype have made this a much easier thing to do in the 21st century.
- Remember that you need to work to build a new community and connections; it takes time and effort and generally is not achieved overnight.

Reflection time 3.2

What strategies can you employ and build into the preparation process to avoid these relationship challenges?

How can you ensure that the communication channels stay open and supportive between you and your organization, partner and family members?

Practical hotspots

Financial challenges

Most people imagine that as an expat on an assignment package they will be comfortably provided for. This might be true but it pays to spend time now analysing the package offered and the cost of living in the proposed location.

While senior executives may be well remunerated for leadership roles, younger assignees relocating for developmental roles may be supported by some of the 'lighter' assignment packages.

Add to this the reality that many dual-income couples become single-income couples on accepting an assignment, at least for a time. It is not difficult to see that financial challenges can occur.

THINKING POINTS:

- Understand the financial impact of a yes decision. Research the cost of living in your host destination and relate this to your expected assignment income.
- Remember to consider all the financial elements of your assignment contract: income, bonuses, allowances for accommodation, pension entitlement and contributions, life assurance and income protection, health insurance, educational funding, partner support, funding for car, etc.
- Understand the tax implications of your relocation and ensure that you are able to access appropriate professional advice and support.
- Build in the cost of the relocation process. Some of this will be subsidized by your organization but remember that setting up a new home can lead to a number of hidden costs.
- Consider your financial back-up plan. What happens in the case of job loss, ill health or death? Consider creating a financial buffer for your personal security.

Educational support

This is an emotive subject for obvious reasons. Getting this wrong can have a huge impact on the relocation experience for all the family.

The following are common hotspots for parents in relation to education:

- not researching the education options and possibilities before saying yes to a relocation opportunity;
- not relocating at the start of the academic year – it can be tougher for the children to integrate midway through a year (although this can sometimes be unavoidable);
- moving to locations where there is huge competition for places in international schools (e.g., Hong Kong);
- thinking that the best-performing school will be the most appropriate for your children – this is not always the case;
- not considering how special needs may be met in the foreign location;
- believing that the only solution is an international school and not considering other options;
- not negotiating the finance and school search support you need to find the best education for your children;
- feeling guilty for causing suffering for the children if they are having trouble adapting to the new school environment; and
- not considering the curriculum differences and so putting your children at a disadvantage longer term.

THINKING POINTS:

- Think about your children's education from their perspective, think about their needs, and then consider the best solution for them. 'Think about the child not the school, turn the issue around. Start from what you know as a parent about your child.'[46]
- Consider all options and the pros and cons of each: local education in the local language, international schools, home schooling, boarding school, etc. Though the first choice is often an international school, local schools can be an option in many countries. The advantage is that your children will integrate into the national culture and if necessary learn the language. Where local education is good there is an increasing tendency for organizations to request that you use local services and to not make funding available for private education.

- Know what education is likely to cost in your host country and either ensure that this is negotiated into your contract or that you will be able to afford it.
- Consider employing an educational consultant to help you to find the best solution for your child.
- Think about how you can include your children in the preparation process so that they feel involved and as though they have some control over their lives. Help them feel comfortable about the choices being made on their behalf.

Healthcare, safety and security

Healthcare is not the same the world over, yet people often forget to think through the health implications of an international move. Here are some of the challenges you should be aware of.

- Healthcare standards and provisions vary from country to country and city to city. Even within the developed world there will be marked differences in accessibility, health systems and processes. If you are relocating to a developing country, then the differences will be even greater. In many countries the state provision will either not be accessible to you or simply not adequate and private healthcare will be a necessity.
- Exposure to diseases will vary from country to country. Tropical countries will heighten your exposure to diseases such as malaria, yellow fever and dengue fever. HIV risks may be greater in some countries due to inadequate blood screening programmes. Some diseases present greater risks to children.
- Immunization requirements will vary, and records are often required for school entry if you have children.
- The treatment of existing conditions may differ, as well as availability of appropriate medication.

You should also consider the security risks associated with the host country. It is easy to think that bad things won't happen to you, but here is an example of how deeply a challenge to your security can affect you. This is a personal story shared by Kristin Louise Duncombe during her interview with the Thriving Abroad Podcast. It is also a story that appears in her book, *Trailing: A Memoir*.

'The other thing that made life in Nairobi difficult is that Nairobi is a quite dangerous place to live. We went through a variety of different criminal things happening to us. I didn't write about all of them in the book because I felt that it would make the book seem too unbelievable. But the one episode that I did highlight, because for me it was very pivotal, was the night that we were violently carjacked. We were basically chased down the road by armed gunmen who tried to kidnap us and they beat up my husband. It wasn't clear whether we were going to make it out alive. And that was a life-changing experience for me because, as I like to say, I'm not the type of person that can get kidnapped by armed gunmen and then just get over it! For me, it kind of destroyed my mental health; whereas my husband – and this is how I refer to him, you might recall, in the book – he's a real cowboy. For him it was a traumatic event, but he got up the next day and went to work, period, the end.'[47]

This is not included to scare you, but to forewarn. There are many places in the world where security can be an issue. You need to ensure you are fully cognizant of the risks and where necessary ensure that appropriate security for your protection is in place.

THINKING POINTS:

- Investigate healthcare in the host country.
- Investigate your organization's private medical healthcare provision. Ensure that it will cover the whole family for all conditions, including pregnancy, childbirth and emergency evacuation.
- Ensure that immunizations are up to date for all the family and investigate what additional vaccinations are required in your host country.
- Consider taking an emergency first-aid course. Whether relocating to a developing country or not, possessing these skills could be life-saving, especially if you're living in a country where you do not speak the language fluently.
- Consider allergies and current medical conditions. How will you maintain treatment and care abroad?
- Take professional advice about security risks if you are concerned about your host country. If it is not a known hotspot for security issues, talk to local colleagues about their impressions of security and safety, the do's and don'ts.

Death

This is something we know you would prefer not to think about. However, we have both seen the sad impact on families when people die abroad unexpectedly.

Consider these points.

- Dying in your host country with no will (intestate) can leave your family vulnerable in terms of their ability to access income and assets at a time when they most need financial support.
- Where the visa permission for a partner/family is dependent on the deceased assignee's work status, the family may be asked to leave the country quickly. At a time when the family members need the stability of their home and friends, they may find themselves having to pack up and leave.
- Dying intestate can take years and significant lawyer's fees to resolve both in the home country and the host country.

THINKING POINTS:

It is not a simple case of creating one will for home country assets and one for host country assets as the wills can interact. There may also be tax consequences. Should you decide to relocate, we recommend seeking the advice of a lawyer who deals with international probate law.

Eldercare

Something to consider when leaving behind those we love is the care of ageing parents. An ageing population in many first-world countries means that knowing how to care for ageing parents while living abroad is becoming more of an issue for international assignees.

Alison Hesketh, owner of TimeFinders, tells the story of one client's eldercare challenge. The client phoned her one day saying:

'I've got a bit of a problem. My father is in hospital in London recovering from brain surgery and my mother is in a completely different hospital, from which she has already escaped twice. Social services have got involved and have told me that my parents are not going to be allowed to go back home. They've said that they're going to send my mother to a specialist dementia unit and my father is going to have to go into a different care home miles away. They're going to forcibly separate them after fifty-odd years of marriage and that's going to kill them. What am I going to do? By the way, I live in Connecticut.'[48]

Dealing with these kinds of situation from home is challenging enough, much worse from thousands of miles away. As Alison says, 'Caring at a distance magnifies those strains a hundred-fold. A happy life abroad can be scuppered by the emotional maelstrom of guilt, resentment, grief and stress.'

THINKING POINTS:

- Consider how you feel about leaving elderly relatives.
- Investigate the support your organization is prepared to provide to help you manage your relatives' care from abroad. Will they cover the cost of emergency flights home, for example?
- Take Alison's advice and have a conversation with your parents about their wishes for care should they become ill and unable to look after themselves. Create a contingency plan that you are able to put into place should an emergency arise.

 Reflection time 3.3

Which of these practical issues resonate with you?

What do you need to know and research to make an informed relocation decisions?

Summary

❑ This chapter has sought to highlight many of the potential challenges. In making your relocation decision, take a balanced view of both the challenges and the opportunities/benefits of relocation for you and your partner/family.

❑ Identify the strategies that will minimize or eliminate the challenges in relation to your:
  - career and professional development;
  - adjustment to your new life abroad;
  - relationships; and
  - practical issues of international relocation.

❑ Complete the pros and cons table in the workbook. Share your thoughts and insights openly and honestly with your partner.

❏ As you consider the challenges, remember that many of them are sur-mountable either through appropriate support from your organization and other support services or through your own resourcefulness. Often, through a mixture of both.

❏ This book and the support from Thriving Abroad is designed to help you make an informed decision and should you choose to go, prepare for a smooth and successful transition to a new life abroad. One that is built on the foundation of a solid understanding of the context, challenges and opportunities of international mobility.

CHAPTER FOUR

The global mobility function

'If we knew what it was we were doing, it would not be called research, would it?'
Albert Einstein

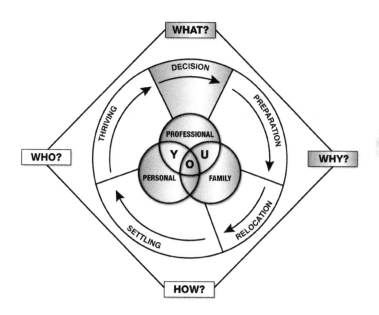

Rich and Angela

Though not one to dwell on regrets, Rich had one that would haunt him long into the future. In his excitement and enthusiasm to embrace their relocation opportunity, he paid scant regard to the terms and conditions of their assignment in terms of organizational support. Looking back, he realized this was because having never relocated abroad before, they had no understanding of their potential support needs; you don't know what you don't know... until it hits you on the head! His company was relatively inexperienced in the international field and no one in head office understood much about the potential challenges either. It was a case of the blind leading the blind. There were so many questions he should have asked, support he should have secured. The admin in setting up their new home had been a nightmare, poor Angela. And now that they had arrived and learned how expensive it was to live in London, he realized he should have thought more about the whole expense side of relocation. It also got him thinking about his other benefits, and his tax situation. It wasn't clear that he was going to get help with that, and then there was his annual bonus and pension – would that still be applicable? He had assumed it would, but perhaps that was a silly mistake on his part. He needed to do some quick thinking and get clarification on a number of things. Then there was Angela's work situation. She seemed to be at a total loss in terms of how to begin the job search process. She needed some help but from where?

Introduction

In negotiating your assignment package and support you need to identify your main priorities and needs and consider how they will be met. We are not suggesting that you'll receive everything that you believe you need in terms of support – there is generally some compromise. But unless you have identified and prioritized what is truly important to you, you may find yourselves under-supported and disappointed, similar to Rich and Angela.

In this chapter, we talk about the relocation experience in terms of the support you can expect from your organization. This is all part of the important information that will help you make an informed decision and lay the foundation for a smooth transition. You will need to consider this support from the perspective of your personal, professional and family life.

Gaining clarity about your support needs and your organization's ability to meet those needs is all about setting realistic expectations and minimizing the chance of disappointment.

In clarifying your understanding of organizational support, you will likely connect with the global mobility function in your organization. Global mobility (GM) is typically a subset of the human resources function. In most international organizations – except perhaps those with a very small number of assignees – GM is responsible for ensuring that international moves happen. In smaller organizations, or ones with few international assignees, a member of the human resource function will probably be responsible for supporting your assignment.

Of course, just as each organization has its own culture, there are huge variations in the way organizations manage GM. Our own experiences reflect this divergence. Several of Evelyn's moves were made with a large multinational company. Policies and procedures for international moves were fully fledged and the level of support was comprehensive. There was established documentation and clear boundaries on compensation and other support. Service providers were mostly well established with clear direction on what they did and did not do. On the other hand, Louise's moves were through a company that rarely initiated international moves and had few established protocols for supporting international assignments. While the company supported some of the basics, Louise and her husband had to do much of the legwork. This meant that time was taken out of the office in the early days to deal with basic settling-in issues, made all the more challenging and time consuming by a lack of understanding of the systems and processes, not to mention the language, in the new location.

Because support for international moves covers such a broad spectrum, it's important to know a bit more about GM and how it works. This chapter will help you to:

- understand what GM will (and won't) do for you;
- begin to identify your own support needs;
- identify the questions you need to ask of your GM partner; and
- discover how to make GM work most effectively for you.

Don't skip this chapter, even if you work for a large company with hundreds of assignees working overseas at the same time. Remember Evelyn's moves with the large multinational? It turned out that their policies and procedures were built around American employees moving abroad. Evelyn and her husband are British and Australian, so significant aspects of the framework didn't apply to them. In addition, Evelyn, unlike many of her peers at the time, did have a career. Evelyn and her husband assumed that because the company had a well-developed process, their situation could be accounted for. They could not have been further from the truth! As the saying goes, 'to assume makes an **ass** out of **u** and **me**', a phrase that Rich in our case study above would probably relate to as well.

What does global mobility do and what does global mobility not do?

In most organizations, GM is responsible for, as one HR director neatly summarized, 'getting international assignees from A to B with the least fuss at the lowest cost'. The reality is considerably more complex. Here's a list of tasks GM will *typically* undertake:

- coordinate with your business unit, the business unit's HR function and the host country's HR function;
- prepare the salary and benefits package for your assignment;
- obtain the appropriate work permits for you and residence permits for you and your family to enable you to work and you and your family to live in your host country;
- ensure that you are compliant with tax laws in both your host and home country and organize tax preparation services for you, although this is not a universal provision;
- organize the physical move to the host country for you, your family and perhaps your pets as well as shipment of some or all of your household goods;
- ensure that you and your family have appropriate medical insurance in your host country;
- ensure that you comply with social security rules and regulations in your host country;
- ensure that your pension rights in your home country are protected to the extent permitted by law;
- help you and your family find appropriate housing in your host country;
- help you and your family find appropriate education in your host country and fund that education if it's private, although this financial provision is not universal;
- ensure you have the support you need in your host country to assist you with practical tasks, such as setting up bank accounts, connecting utilities, etc.
- provide you and your partner (and perhaps older children) with language classes;
- provide you and your partner (and perhaps older children) with cross-cultural training; and
- refer you to appropriate resources or service providers to obtain advice or services for other aspects of your move.

Equally important is to be aware of the tasks for which GM departments are typically not responsible, though some may provide certain assistance:

- deciding whether you are the right person for the assignment – this is usually the responsibility of human resources, and functional or line management, such as the business unit with the resourcing need;
- negotiating the magnitude of your salary and benefits;
- making policy exceptions to meet your individual needs – increasingly, organizations are standardizing their policy provisions, which means there may be limited flexibility for personal needs; however, some organizations favour a more flexible style of benefit provision whereby an overall budget is provided and assignees are able to choose the benefits that most meet their needs;
- conducting performance reviews while you are in post;
- providing ongoing career management or identifying your next assignment;
- providing complete information regarding your partner's right to work and ability to find a job;
- obtaining work permits for spouses and partners, although some organizations will consider this support on a discretionary basis;
- helping spouses and partners to find employment in the host country;
- identifying and providing the training or mentoring needed to facilitate your in-post performance;
- helping you to identify resources and/or funding special educational or medical needs;
- helping you to identify extracurricular sports and creative resources for you or your children.

How does global mobility work?

It's also helpful to understand how your GM services might be delivered, as this also varies from company to company.

In-house or outsourced?

It is rare that your entire relocation will be handled by people who work for your company. Companies are increasingly outsourcing aspects of the GM process. Some companies will outsource only those elements that require highly specialized skills and knowledge, such as immigration and taxation services, while others will outsource almost the entire process to one of several large relocation firms. Regardless of the level of outsourcing, you are likely to have a GM contact who is responsible for overseeing the process.

Host HR and destination services

An important element of relocation is the services provided to help you get situated in your new country. These services are typically provided by either local HR within your host country or by an outsourced destination services provider. Regardless of how these services are provided, they will be important when it comes to making decisions about where to live and where your children might go to school, and in navigating local bureaucracy. Generally, these services will provide help with house hunting, school searching, setting up appropriate utilities and registering for provisions such as medical services. They will normally be provided for a set number of hours or days. A small number of organizations provide only contact and self-help information, as was the case for Louise.

Policies and exceptions

As in HR generally, GM packages and procedures are usually governed by a set of policies that ensure everyone is dealt with fairly. This can be somewhat complex as certain benefits may vary according to personal circumstances, such as family size. Exceptions to policy are not made easily in most organizations, and GM may not have the authority to make them. There may also be a different range of policies and provisions for different kinds of assignment: developmental, leadership, technical and short-term, for example.

In-post HR

Once your move is complete and you are working in your new job in your host country, GM will take a back seat and a business or local HR professional will be responsible for you. However, GM may continue to be involved in the administration of your benefits and legal status, and in some cases may have a role in identifying your next career move.

What questions do you need to ask your global mobility partners?

If you've never been on an international assignment before, understanding how the GM process will work can be a minefield. You may not even know what questions to ask. The following section outlines some of the key questions you should ask your GM partner in order to understand how your compensation package will look and what support you will get and from where. It will also help you to understand what additional support you might need. We'll talk about some of these in more detail in future chapters, but this list should be sufficient to help you navigate the GM process.

1. **Which country will be my home base for compensation purposes?**
   It's important that you understand whether you will be considered as
   based in your home or host country by your company. 'Home country'
   refers to the country where your contract of employment was originally based. Typically, home-based employees receive benefits that
   enable them to replicate their standard of living in their home country, whereas local-based employees will not; this can either work in
   your favour or against you, depending on the country or your personal
   circumstances.
   - Local Plus is a hybrid of the two, meaning that you are consid-
     ered a local employee in your host country but might receive some
     additional benefits, such as an allowance for school fees if it's not
     appropriate for your children to go into the local system. Whether
     you are home or host based may also affect how you are treated
     by your company for tax purposes, as home-based employees will
     typically be tax equalized so that they receive neither a penalty nor
     a windfall from taxes.
   - If your policy is home-based then the compensation package will
     be based on compensation for the equivalent job in your home
     country and designed to keep you 'whole' in relation to life in the
     home country. As a result, a home-based package may contain
     elements such as an allowance for housing, school fees and cost
     of living, applied to ensure that your salary's purchasing power is
     maintained abroad. Assignees on a home-based package are usu-
     ally tax equalized to their home country. These packages are more
     costly and difficult to administer and are becoming less common
     as more people become globally mobile. More organizations are
     now choosing to use the Local Plus approach.
2. **What are the full terms of my assignment?** It is important to under-
   stand the details on which your assignment policy of support is based.
   - What will be the duration of your assignment?
   - How will you be remunerated and to what level, in terms of salary,
     annual increases and performance reviews and bonus payments?
   - What additional benefits will you be entitled to and how will your
     international status affect them? Consider here your pension, life
     assurance and sickness benefits, including medical insurance. Sup-
     port for private education has traditionally been provided, but
     where the state education is judged to be satisfactory, such support
     may not be available.
   - Are there additional benefits? These may include a miscellaneous
     or settling-in allowance, expressed as a percentage of salary or one
     month's salary to support you through the transition period and

assist with the additional costs of relocation. In some locations, you
may be entitled to a hardship allowance.

- What provision is made for language and cross-cultural training
  support for you, your partner and family?
- Will the organization secure the appropriate visas for your partner
  and family, including a working visa if your partner wishes to work
  while abroad?
- What additional support packages or allowances are available for
  your partner should they wish to seek work or pursue new educational or professional interests? Don't leave any stones unturned
  – evaluate your support package in the same way you would if you
  were changing companies.

3. **What services will be provided for me and by whom?** Ensure you
   understand fully what both GM and external service providers will do
   for you – who will be responsible and for what provisions and services.
   As we discuss below, understanding the answer to this question will
   facilitate a better working relationship and will also ensure that you
   don't miss out on services which might help you.

4. **How can GM help me to meet specific needs that are not addressed
   in the service package?** You may find that your personal circumstances require services other than those provided. While GM may
   not be able to provide these services, they may be able to help you to
   identify someone who can. Finding a local mentor is often a great place
   to start, and one that the local host company could possibly supply or
   assist with.

Of course, as you get into the process of moving, you will identify more detailed
questions, and to get those answered, it's important to build a productive relationship with your GM providers.

 Reflection time 4.0

*What issues has this section prompted you to investigate as you begin your con-
versations with GM about your assignment terms and conditions?*

Working with your global mobility function

As we mentioned above, there are huge variations between organizations
regarding the way that GM services are delivered, what is included in relocation packages and how assignees are dealt with from an HR perspective while
on assignment. The earlier part of this chapter should have given you enough
information to be able to ask the right questions, but there is more you can do
to ensure that you get the best out of your GM process.

Building a productive relationship with global mobility

Moving internationally can be stressful, and your relationships with the people tasked with helping you can either be positive or negative forces in getting you through it. We have seen the relationship between assignee family and GM provider become extremely combative, which serves only to exacerbate an already emotionally charged and stressful situation. Of course, it takes two to build a relationship and there are some things that you can do to help your relationship with GM stay on an even keel.

Build appropriate expectations

One of the biggest causes of friction in the international relocation is a mismatch between expectations and reality. A lack of clarity leads to miscommunication and misunderstanding which in turn leads to tasks being missed and delays in the process. The consequences almost always impact the assignee and family.

- Have a clear understanding up front of who is responsible for what tasks.
- If you have a circumstance that may be challenging to deal with or may need special resources (e.g., your partner's job, a child with special needs), raise the issue as early in the process as possible so you can make a plan with GM to address it.
- Be prepared to do your own research, particularly on issues that are important to you or if your situation is out of the ordinary. Don't expect your GM team to know everything. They don't, and expecting they do can only lead to problems.
- Don't expect everyone in the process to understand the experience. Many people involved in your relocation will be relatively junior and may not have lived or worked abroad themselves.
- Make sure you know what GM is expecting of you and your family in the process.

Making the most of the resources you have

Assignees and their families often discover after the fact that one service provider or another could have offered much-needed support on an issue if only they'd known to ask. You can avoid that situation by asking up front for a clear outline of what services will be provided by whom. If you have an issue that is important, ask at the start of the process what support you will get for it. It's particularly important to ask in regard to outsourced services as service providers are less likely to understand your circumstances and will be relying on information passed on from GM. Moreover, because service contracts are negotiated very tightly, service providers have no real incentive to 'go the extra mile' and may assume that unless you ask, you don't need a particular service.

Making sure you get the support you need

The support package you are offered may not include all necessary support. We have seen this is particularly the case in terms of work permits and career assistance for spouses and partners, but it could also affect a special circumstance you have. Of course, the first port of call should be your organization – ask if they will provide the support you need. However, if your organization is not able, be prepared to seek it out and pay for it yourself. While the short-term saving of, say, not getting appropriate advice regarding what is required to get a spouse or partner work permit may feel attractive, the long-term consequences of not getting the right advice or support can be far reaching.

Ongoing global mobility support

Once you and your family are in your host country, GM may play a role in helping you to get settled, often through a destination services provider charged with helping you to manage the bureaucratic process (e.g., setting up utilities, bank accounts, etc). Your destination services provider may also be able to help you and your family find practical services such as doctors, dentists, etc. However, you may find that you are more comfortable relying on other families you meet for those recommendations. Beyond initial settling in, your interactions with GM will be few. You will more likely be supported by local HR in your host country and/or the HR group assigned to your business unit. GM will work in the background as they are likely to have responsibility for administering your compensation and any allowances you receive. GM may also become involved if you have a change of circumstance while in post. Depending on the extent to which GM in your organization is involved in talent management and development, they may or may not be involved in supporting your next move. Your proactive role in that process is something we'll discuss in later chapters.

This chapter has given you an overview of the GM function – what it does and how it might work. You should have enough information to take a proactive role in your own relocation; ask the right questions so that you're clear on how to get the support you need and how you'll make the most of that support.

 Reflection time 4.1

What is your strategy for working effectively with GM?

Summary

- ❑ GM typically sits within the HR function.

- ❑ GM is responsible for a range of tasks designed to get assignees to their location with the least fuss at the lowest cost.

- ❑ Your move may be managed fully by the GM function or outsourced.

- ❑ Cost containment is increasingly a key objective of GM.

- ❑ Organizations are increasingly focusing more on collecting and analysing data on assignees and their performance.

- ❑ GM policies are becoming more inclusive.

- ❑ Talent management processes are becoming more integrated into GM.

- ❑ Organizations are moving away from paternalistic policies to those that encourage empowerment, self-reliance and responsibility.

CHAPTER FIVE

Should I stay or should I go?

'Nothing happens until you decide. Make a decision and watch your
life move forward.'
Oprah Winfrey

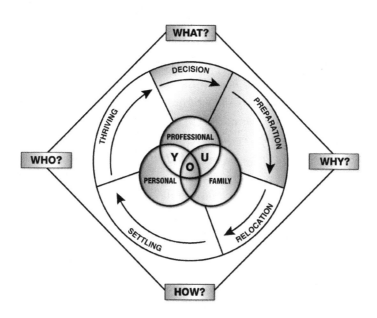

Jenny and Paul

Five months into their new lives in Shanghai, Jenny had returned exhausted from a business trip to find Paul in a foul mood. Recalling this moment, Jenny remembered how puzzled she had felt. As she had flown home, looking forward to a family weekend, she had reflected that finally things were beginning to feel more settled. She had survived the baptism by fire in terms of starting her new job, the children had made friends and were enjoying their new school and activities and Paul seemed happy, although somewhat jaded, by the amount of time he was spending 'home alone' while she was away on business trips. The extent of her travel schedule had come as a bit of a surprise, but there had been little she could do about it. So, walking in and being met by Paul's bad temper had been a bit of a shock – normally they both looked forward to the weekends, and typically there would be an excited and welcoming family awaiting her. This time, the children had already been tucked up in bed and Paul, after a perfunctory kiss on the cheek, had said he needed to talk to her. Jenny went off to change to buy herself a bit of time and calm herself down. After the week she'd just had, this was tough to take. She counted to ten and went to face the music. Paul, it transpired, had had enough. He wanted them to go home. He was missing his career, his colleagues and his life. Being a househusband and full-time stay-at-home dad was not his thing. Jenny was shocked at his strength of feeling but not surprised. He had made it clear at the outset that while he was happy to take a short career break to help everyone settle in, he wanted a professional outlet while abroad. Jenny realized she needed to let Paul vent, and sat and listened as he shared how he was feeling. The latest job rejection was what had ignited this reaction. Understandable. Once Paul had calmed down, Jenny gently brought him back to the decision they had made – the commitment they had both made to make it work. They had a plan after all, and they were only five months in. Someone had suggested that they record their decision, and their reasons for accepting this move. She found it, and they reminded themselves of the foundations of that decision. Paul relaxed; his professional life was a part of the picture, an important one, but so was the value of the experience for everyone. They were achieving positive outcomes in pretty much every other area of importance to them. His job was the only true blip, and frustrating as it was, it would change. Jenny promised to help and support him as he re-thought the opportunities China presented professionally for him.

Introduction

The decision that you're facing is a life-impacting one for everyone concerned: assignee, partner and family. The way in which the decision is made, the issues considered, and the actions taken will lay the foundations for your experience abroad.

Without doubt some people make a reactive and insufficiently considered and researched decision to relocate internationally. This may be because they are attracted by the excitement and adventure, or they are pushed by the assigning organization to make a quick decision because of pressing business needs. Consequences may include:

- decisions that they live to regret;
- due to a poor understanding of challenges and needs, poorly negotiated contracts of employment that feature gaps and inadequacies in the different forms of support, causing stress and contention once abroad;
- a partner who follows and drifts into a new life abroad with little or no buy-in, potentially leading to resentment and frustration abroad, and perhaps a demand to return home early;
- no sense of responsibility for the success of the relocation experience; and
- at the extreme, relationship breakdown leading to separation and divorce.

Ingolf Thom, Global HR Director for Dow Chemical Company, said in a conversation that 'people don't know what they don't know. The decision to move overseas is a more complicated decision than the decision to change companies, and yet few people do as much homework and they are often forced to make a decision in a very short time.'

We encourage you to take the time to make a well-informed and proactive decision. If you feel under pressure to make a fast decision by your organization then ask for time to consider it more fully. With the cost of an assignment equating to two or three times your salary, it is in everyone's interest that your decision is one you feel motivated by and happy about.

This suggestion to take time to think through the decision is not so much based on the risk of failure or a wrong choice; rather, it's based more on the fact that if you understand the opportunities and challenges, you'll be better prepared for the experience. You will embark on your expat journey with realistic expectations. This understanding can enhance your overall experience.

If you have already made the decision to move, work through this chapter to clarify your personal motivations for going. This chapter will also help you to identify the personal resources available to help carry you forward.

Equally, if you've decided that your answer is no, you will understand the reasons for that choice.

The Five Pillars decision-making process

The Five Pillars model will ensure that your decision is a sound one.

Of course you cannot predict everything, but the more you research and understand the opportunity and your personal and professional objectives in relation to the decision, the better.

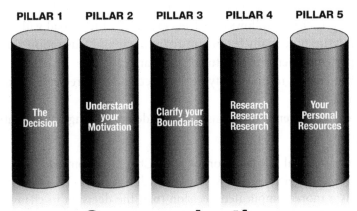

The Five Pillars decision-making process

- **Pillar One: Define your decision**
  What is your decision about? Define it and agree that this is the decision you will be making jointly with your partner.

- **Pillar Two: Understand your motivation**
  What attracts and motivates you to make this life change?

- **Pillar Three: Clarify your boundaries**
  What has to be in place for this to work for you?

- **Pillar Four: Research, research, research**
  Understand what you need to know to make an informed decision and get researching.

- **Pillar Five: Your personal resources**
  What do you bring to the experience that will enable you to perform effectively and live enjoyably in your new location?

The running theme throughout the process is communication. Your decision needs to be based on open and honest communication between you and your partner/family, your employer, and your host country employer/colleagues.

How to decide

Should your decision be based on an emotional gut feeling, fate, luck and/or deep thought and introspection? Does the method you use to make the decision impact on your success abroad?

There is little research that relates how the relocation decision is made to the success of the assignment. However, there is research that identifies factors that contribute to expatriate success, and one of these factors is realistic expectations.

One reason given for poor adjustment to a new life abroad is that the reality of the experience does not match up to expectations. In order to have realistic expectations, you need to understand what you want and need in your new life abroad and know how your proposed relocation will match those wants and needs.

Research shows that high-value decisions are often made through an intensely cognitive process: people have thought about what they want, their buying criteria, and then matched the selection of those goods to the most important criteria.[49] We encourage you to think about your relocation in this way.

It isn't a totally rational process though. There is an emotional and contextual aspect to the decision as well. We asked people in an online poll[50] how they made their relocation decision, and methods ranged from rational, clearly thought out processes encompassing research and analysis of the pros and cons to predominantly emotional decisions based on a gut feeling. Some mixed both the rational with a gut feeling and came to a consensus opinion; for others, the decision was based on a long-term desire (almost a pre-decision decision) to live abroad at some point in their lives.

Only you will know how deeply you feel you need to research and analyse before making your relocation decision. We recommend a mix of methods. Consider both the objective and the subjective factors. To that end, we suggest a blend of analytical and intuitive thinking. This needs to be based on research that is focused and relevant. Let your life experiences, beliefs and attitudes inform your decision, and come to a conclusion based on as much evidence and consensus of opinion as you can.

This brings us to our last point. Consensus of opinion. In our poll, 12% of assignees said that the decision rested with them; 22% of the expat partners completing the survey said that as their partner was the main breadwinner, they didn't feel that they had any choice and needed to go where their partner's work opportunities existed. One participant wrote, 'Even when I said no, my partner went ahead and went, first as an interim manager but of course he was offered the job, by then I didn't have a choice anymore.'

We say make it your objective to reach a joint and informed decision. This is one of the most important foundational aspects of a healthy relocation experience.

Time to get started.

Pillar One: Define your decision

What exactly is the decision that you are making? We know that people reading this book will be making decisions from different perspectives and start points. For example, you may be deciding whether:

- international assignments are of interest to you and your family generally before asking to be added to an assignment pool or considered for future opportunities;
- a relocation opportunity in a role that has arisen out of the blue is attractive – is it attractive and of interest to you, and do you want to relocate abroad?
- one location or role is more attractive than alternatives presented at the same time;
- your desire for international experience is more important than your partner's current career trajectory; and
- you want to take one assignment and then return home or become more internationally mobile by taking a series of international relocations.

 Reflection time 5.0

Think about the decision you are making; identify and agree on the decision to be made with your partner.

Pillar Two: Understand your motivation

What makes changing your life completely and moving to live in a new location, perhaps halfway across the world, attractive?

What motivates you to relocate to live your life abroad?

Research by Glassock and Fee into the relocation decision-making processes of self-initiated expatriates identified 43 motivations, which can be divided into:[51]

- adventure/travel;
- career;
- money;
- escape/life change; and
- family/personal relations.

Generally, the motivation for international relocation is complex. People are motivated by multiple factors, as this excerpt from the above research demonstrates:

'After working in the same job for ten years, respondent #04 felt work was becoming "mundane" and wanted to "do something different" (escape). He saw an opportunity to earn "four times what I was earning here" by working in England (money), but also wanted to "see more of the world and travel around Europe" with his young family (adventure and travel). He viewed expatriation as a way of achieving all these goals simultaneously.'[51]

Think about why you are motivated to relocate abroad considering the five motivations listed below. We also consider a sixth, the role of serendipity or gut reactions.

Adventure and travel

This is often cited as a reason for relocation and a benefit of relocating abroad. In a survey of over 300 expat partners conducted by Thriving Abroad in 2012,[52] this view was reflected by many respondents. They appreciated the opportunity that living abroad gave them to see the world and benefit from the learning that new experiences gave them. They also talked about the challenge, adventure, fun and personal enjoyment gained from the experience.

Career

As a potential international assignee, you must consider your career in the decision. What motivates you about the opportunity that an international role provides? Think about the work role satisfaction, enhanced career development, and opportunity for personal development, as outlined in Chapter One. For many international assignees, career development is a persuasive reason for accepting an international position.

However, in every job change there is an element of risk, and this is enhanced when it's an international role. The work-related experience may not go as planned for any number of reasons and the return to the home location may be disappointing. While taking a proactive stance to manage the experience as positively as possible can reduce the chance of poor assignment outcomes, it is still a risk, and one you should acknowledge.

As the expat partner, think about the impact of international relocation on your career. What expectations do you have in relation to your career abroad? How realistic are these expectations? Research the practical aspects, such as access to a work visa, recognition of qualifications and job search support, before making the decision to relocate. Also consider how you feel about career reinvention.

Money

There are split opinions about the financial benefits of relocation. As organizations focus on controlling GM budgets, expatriates still talk about the positive financial implications of being globally mobile.

According to the GM practitioners that we interviewed, benefit packages are designed to provide a similar standard of living in the new location (compared to the home location) – to keep people whole, not make them rich.

Also, assignees who focus on the financial opportunity of GM at the expense of other career-related considerations set alarm bells ringing in the minds of GM professionals. These professionals understand that the extrinsic motivation provided by financial compensation is not as strong as the intrinsic motivation that comes from the desire to relocate for personal and professional developmental and experiential reasons.

Escape and life change

Today, many people are escaping from economic and political hardship as these comments from our decision survey demonstrate.

- 'Escape crime and violence of South Africa.'
- 'Was unemployed and needed a job. The job I was offered was abroad.'
- 'The Spanish Crisis.'

Others, like Paul and Jenny, talk about a desire for general life change, a desire to try something new before settling down in a way that would make relocation difficult in the future. Partners sometimes tell us that they were keen to relocate to leave jobs and take a career break. Employees may apply for assignment opportunities to escape work-related issues back home. Some couples see the opportunity to relocate as the new start that will resolve relationship issues.

Obviously, some of these choices are healthier than others. Running away from personal issues, or at least trying to, is never a good solution. Where personal relationships are concerned the problems tend to travel too, and are generally exacerbated by the relocation challenges rather than ameliorated.

Consider what you are escaping from and think forward in time. How will relocation affect what you are escaping from one month down the line? One year? Five years?

Family and personal relationships

Seeking a personal or family adventure is another non-financial reason for GM. The benefit of international experience for the family was mentioned many times in our research.[53] It is certainly a compelling reason, but it is important to consider this within the context of the whole opportunity. Ask yourself the following questions.

- Is the career move a sensible one for everyone in the family, or are we being blindsided by the opportunity for international adventure?
- How big a challenge will this be for our children and is it the right time for them to relocate from an educational perspective?
- What are the safety and security implications of such a move for all the family?
- What is the impact on the extended family? How do we feel about leaving them behind, and how will we manage the care of elderly relatives from afar?

Serendipity and gut reaction

Often there is an element of serendipity that is involved in relocation decisions. In our online poll, respondents used phrases such as 'we considered ourselves lucky' or 'we decided to take a chance and it worked out'. For some people, 'jobs fell into their laps'. Others decided to take risks.

What is important is that you are clear about the factors that motivate *your* decision. It's personal after all! Is it based on career motivation and/or the desire for an international adventure or some other combination of factors?

Your motivation becomes your reason why – your inner compass charting your course, and the purpose behind your decision.

Reflection time 5.1

Identify your core motivations and goals for international mobility.

If you are relocating with a partner, some motivations may be joint and some, individual. All should be discussed and acknowledged.

Pillar Three: Clarify your boundaries

In pillar three you think about what you will need the experience to provide in order for it to work for you and your partner.

When negotiating your assignment contract, you will need to know what absolutely has to happen for the experience to work for you. This means that you need to 'clarify your boundaries'.

In order to understand your boundaries you have to understand your needs. Think about your three life areas (personal, professional and family) and identify what is most important for you in each. For example, in relation to family, you may identify the following as important:

- education for my children;
- annual visits home to see my family; and
- weekends spent with my family.

The value in understanding what is important in each area is that you can then create a list of requirements in relation to family. For example, there must be:

- good educational possibilities and funding;
- annual subsidized trips home for all the family; and
- an agreement that business travel/work commitments are confined predominantly to weekdays.

It is important to recognize that not everything will be possible. There will be points of compromise. One way to ensure that you are compromising on the right things is to create a master list of everything that is important to you and then prioritize the items within that list into a) non-negotiables (absolute musts), b) musts (but you'd survive without if necessary) and c) nice-to-haves (bonuses).

 Reflection time 5.2

Clarify what you want or need in your personal, professional and family life for this assignment to be successful.

Compare your list with your partner's and agree on your priority list.

Pillar Four: Research, research, research

One of the most common reasons for expatriate dissatisfaction is unmet expectations. While it is impossible to know absolutely everything about the relocation experience or plan for every eventuality and challenge, it is sensible to develop your understanding of the opportunity. It is easy to make assumptions, but don't be tempted. Assumptions lead to false and dashed expectations. Research:

- the basis on which you are relocating, the job role and the support package;
- the location to which you are moving from a geographical, practical and cultural perspective; and
- the challenges and opportunities presented by international relocation.

One way of researching is to take a familiarization visit to the proposed location. Familiarization visits typically last between three and five days. They are a chance to get to know the new location – visit the company, schools, potential accommodation. Ensure that the decision made is based on a full understanding of the locational aspects of the assignment.

Research can also be conducted online. We give a list of some useful websites in the resources section of this book.

Remember that expats already living in your target location will be able to provide you with up-to-date information.

Hopefully you developed a list of research questions as you read through the first four chapters of the book. Now, focus on finding answers and building the knowledge base on which you will make your relocation decision and prepare to move abroad.

 Reflection time 5.3

What research do you need to do to answer the questions you have about the potential relocation experience in relation to each area of your life?
- *Personal*
- *Professional*
- *Family*

Pillar Five: Your personal resources

The expat experience will take you out of your comfort zone and then some. This is part of the attraction for many people, and good news from a personal growth and developmental perspective. It is helpful to think about the personal and practical resources that might support you through an international relocation.

An analysis of your personal resources will help you identify where you need to develop skills and knowledge – for example, language, cultural intelligence and global mindset. We rarely move into new roles that we are 100% equipped to perform. Personal and professional development is a given if we are being stretched to work within new roles and environments.

Understanding your personal skills, strengths and talents is also a great confidence booster.

Personal resources

- What skills and knowledge do you possess? Refer to past work roles, performance reviews, development programmes and assessments; note your accomplishments, achievements, abilities and skill sets. Identifying these things will give you great insight into what you do well. Then consider how you'll be able to use your skills and knowledge as you plan, relocate and adjust to your new life abroad.
- What is your general attitude to life? There are people who see the glass half empty and those who see it half full. Which are you?
- Refer back to the skills outlined in Chapter Two. When have you already had an opportunity to develop and use these skills? How can you continue to use and develop them in this new role and international experience?
- What are your personal strengths? You possess many – they are what make you uniquely you. Utilizing these in your daily activities, both personal and professional, means that you will perform better and be more engaged and enthusiastic about what you are doing.
- For the assignee, consider the role that you will be undertaking, if you know at this stage, and think about your personal fit. Where would you benefit from additional support? Language acquisition? Cross-cultural training and coaching? Executive coaching and support?
- For the partner, consider what skills you will need to develop to live comfortably in your new environment and pursue the activities, interests and/or career that you wish to while abroad. Where will you benefit from additional support?

Practical resources

Think about the practical resources that you have or have access to that will support you as you make this transition:

- financial resources;
- family support;
- organizational support (GM specialists) and professional support (tax, legal and immigration advice);
- access to expats and advice in your destination location and people you know who have lived abroad; and
- mentors and/or coaches.

Reflection time 5.4

What personal resources will support you through the transition process to the creation of your success abroad?

Communication

Communication is central to the whole decision-making process and to your success abroad. Jenny and Paul seemed to be experiencing a bit of a breakdown in their communication. However, the potential negative fallout of Paul's bad mood and experience was avoided because they took time to sit down and talk and listen to each other. They revisited their mutual understanding of their original motivation for relocating. Their experience underlines the value of a joint, agreed and recorded decision between two partners. It is not healthy or positive when a relocation decision starts with one partner feeling resentment towards the other.

Think about the ways you will develop and sustain open communication with your partner, children and extended family. Communicate with your employer and colleagues and ensure you sustain those open communication channels once you are abroad.

Remember that communication is the basis on which relationships are built – or broken.

The following is an excerpt from a Thriving Abroad podcast interview with Jacquie Kane, Director of Strategic Marketing and Communications at School Year Abroad. She shares her reaction to an opportunity to move to China in support of her husband's career.

'There were some tough conversations that my husband and I had. I think in most cases, it is the husband, in some cases the wife, that's driving the decision to pursue their career abroad. I really loved the firm that I worked for, doing very meaningful work with clients that I loved, colleagues that I enjoyed working with, so I was initially very reluctant to walk away from something that I'd worked very hard for. I had established myself and saw a career path continuing where I was.

I think, for many accompanying partners in that position, it's almost like an initial struggle between the over-ambitious partner who wants to grasp that opportunity and the partner that then starts to look at loss and think about compromise in order to support their partner's career. . . . And I think it's an important conversation to have with your partner, because you do have to sit down and assess what's the benefit to you, to your career, to your life; how can you make the most of this opportunity. And I think it's about having that frank conversation.

Once I'd started doing some research… and my husband was very help-ful in connecting me with the head of PR for his global firm, so I could ask a few questions and suss out the lay of the land, I was able to turn it around and say, "You know what? This is two years out of our life and this could be the making of us. And if we've the courage to grasp this opportunity and if I really focus on what I want to get out of this next two years, I can make this an amazing opportunity for myself – or I can sit in the high rise and bemoan everything that I've left behind and alienate myself, rather than embrace this experience.

So, it's about having the correct positive mindset to say, "Yes, this is not what I would have wished for myself in terms of a life plan. However, this is an opportunity that, in ten years' time, we're going to reflect on and say, 'That was the most incredible transformative experience, and I'm so glad that I took the risk to leave the familiar behind and slip out of my comfort zone and really push myself to see if I can do this.'" And I just developed that mindset very quickly and said, "Let's do it.""

Decision time

Hopefully working through the Five Pillars helped you to consider your issues of importance. Following your research, you will have a solid sense of what your life could be like abroad, and what you want to achieve both personally and professionally.

Now it's time to pull together all the different elements of the decision and answer the question that you identified in Pillar One: Define your decision.

Here we suggest some exercises to help you come to your final decision. Spend some time playing with the questions and see what comes out for you. You may want to work on them over several days, even over several weeks if you have the time. Then, once you have your thoughts consolidated, it will be decision time!

Reflection time 5.5

Complete the following exercises.

Exercise One: Consolidate your thinking

Answer these questions. If you are making a joint decision, do this separately first and then come together to combine and discuss your answers.

- What is this opportunity about from a purely factual perspective?
- What is your *gut* reaction to this opportunity?
- How do you *feel* when you think about this opportunity?
- What are your *positive and optimistic ideas/thoughts* about this opportunity, now and for the future?
- What are your *negative and pessimistic ideas/thoughts* about this opportunity, now and for the future?
- Close your eyes and imagine that you are already living in this new location. What does your life look like?

Now share what you have written with your partner.

- Where do you agree?
- Where do you disagree?
- What points of contention exist?
- What can be done to overcome them?

Exercise Two: Opportunities and threats

Draw two columns on a page and label one 'Opportunities' and the other 'Threats'. Ask yourself:

- What are the opportunities?
- What are the threats?

And then ask, what is the worst-case scenario? What is the worst thing that could happen if this all went wrong? What impact would that have professionally, personally and financially?

Finally, ask, what is the best-case scenario? What could happen that would be really positive? What impact would that have professionally, personally and financially?

Exercise Three: Where does this decision take you?

Imagine if you say *yes* what you will be doing and thinking in five weeks, five months and five years (choose any timescale that is meaningful for you).

The Decision:

Time to decide yes or no. If you are making a joint decision, ensure you have completed the three exercises above independently and then compare your answers.

- How do you feel about these answers?
- Do you have a decision?
- Is this an agreed decision?

Exercise Four: Summary document

Like Paul and Jenny did, we recommend you write a summary document consolidating the main factors influencing your decision. It should include the following.

- Our joint decision is...
- We are motivated to make this decision because...
- Our longer-term personal and professional aspirations are...
- Our reasons for yes/no are...
- The following needs and requirements are non-negotiable and will have to be met in order for us to make this a reality...
- We would like the following needs and requirements to be met, although we can be flexible...
- Our personal and practical resources are...

Then both partners should sign the document. It represents the foundation of your international experience.

This book now moves forward to support people who decide *yes*. Not everyone will decide yes. You might conclude that the current opportunity is not the right one, or that international relocation generally is not right for you at this point in your life.

If your answer is no, this process will still have been a positive one for you. In helping you to define what you don't want, it will have helped you to define what you do want. Use this decision as the basis for your next steps as you work to create a future that you love.

This one decision is the beginning of many more. While we hope that this process helped you to make the relocation decision, we believe that the basic principles in the process will provide a template for many future decisions, both big and small.

Summary

- ❑ The decision process is structured around Five Pillars.
  - ◆ **Pillar One:** What decision are you making? Clearly define it and agree upon it.
  - ◆ **Pillar Two:** Identify and agree on your primary motivations for relocating internationally.
  - ◆ **Pillar Three:** Know what is important to you and clarify your relocation boundaries.
  - ◆ **Pillar Four:** Ensure that your decision is based on a full understanding of the facts in all areas that are important to you. Remember, assumptions lead to false expectations.
  - ◆ **Pillar Five:** Our sense of personal competence affects our confidence. Understand your personal and practical resources. Know where you need to ask for help and support.

- ❑ **The Decision:** Make an informed, joint and conscious decision and record your reasons why.

PART TWO

Making It Happen

CHAPTER SIX

The logistics of moving – more than fitting life into a box

'By failing to prepare you are preparing to fail.'
Benjamin Franklin

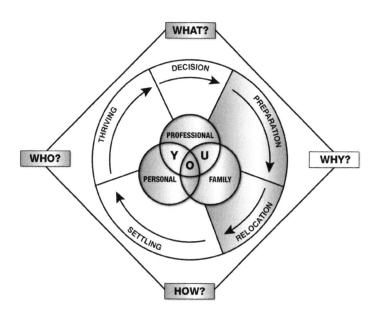

Rich and Angela

It still gave Angela nightmares to think about how they organized and prepared for the move. It had been utterly chaotic. The fact that they had arrived at all was a miracle. As their departure date drew nearer, they threw themselves into a flurry of unfocused activity. In truth, neither of them had given much thought to the preparation. Sure, they'd talked about letting their house, but not much more. Suddenly, with four weeks to go, the reality of what needed to be done hit home. How could they have been so blasé? Rich's company had started the visa process, fortunately. Now they realized they should have prioritized finding a home, but how to do that from the other side of the Atlantic? They decided to buy time and opted to stay in a hotel for the first weeks, but finding something suitable in a decent part of London for a reasonable price was almost impossible. Rich negotiated an extra allowance, but that would only be available for three weeks. They also needed to rent out their home, get rid of the car, sort out furniture and decide what to ship to the UK. Their finances, which were all over the place, needed to be consolidated. As Angela was not going to be working in the UK, it was decided she would manage their finances while abroad. It seemed strange to her to manage money that she didn't feel was hers in a country where she was not working and initially didn't even have a postal address. In retrospect, the chaos resulted from the lack of any organizing system. Every evening during their last weeks at home, they would argue over who should have done what. The icing on the cake came when Angela was informed by the visa company that she only had five months to run on her passport.

After you decide to accept an international assignment and relocation, your focus must turn to preparation for the move. The way that families prepare their relocation can make a critical difference in the early days of the assignment and can impact its long-term success. A family thoroughly prepared for an assignment is more likely to have a positive and empowering relocation experience, whereas those whose preparation has been less comprehensive often face unpleasant surprises and a difficult start to their new lives.

This chapter addresses two of the biggest issues that inhibit the preparation process. The first is lack of time. Few families have the luxury of months to prepare. They are usually juggling busy work and personal lives, and preparing for the move is one more project to be squeezed into an already hectic schedule. The second issue is that people who have never moved before don't know what they don't know. Preparing well means addressing issues you might not have known existed. These are exactly the issues that, unaddressed, can lead to unpleasant surprises and unintended consequences.

By the end of this chapter, you'll be ready to launch a preparation process that will set you up for the best possible start to your move. This chapter will:

- help you to create an effective system for organizing the myriad aspects of your move; and
- pinpoint the issues that are important to address, including the ones often overlooked in the preparation process.

Create a system to prepare for the logistics of the move

Evelyn's made six international moves. In the course of making all of those moves, she refined her system and methodology for keeping on top of what might otherwise be an overwhelming project, with each move more complex than the last one.

In this section, we share Evelyn's methodology and some of our key insights so you can organize your move in the most comprehensive and efficient way possible.

Get ready for the project

One of the hardest parts of organizing an international move is keeping control of the mountain of information, paperwork and research. Containing it all is a critical first step. Decide how and where you're going to store all the information you need. Keep in mind the multiple formats in which information comes to you, and make sure you have a place or places to store information on paper, in digital documents and in e-mails; bookmark websites that contain useful information. That way, you'll know exactly where to find all your information quickly.

Get the contents of your brain on paper

Our brains are not good at multitasking. In fact, when you think you are multitasking, you are most likely task-switching. This means you're really paying attention to only one task at a time. If your brain is constantly cycling through your mental 300-item to-do list, you are not giving as much attention as you could to the things you are working on. Getting your list out of your head is the best way to remove the 'I must remember' loop going on in your brain. Make a list of everything you need to do in one place – you can work out priorities, how to get things done and who does them later.

Create a timeline and priorities

The next step is making a timeline so you can deal with deadlines in a timely manner. Deadlines relating to schools and housing tend to be particularly important. Even if you have support from your company, don't rely on a third party to meet those deadlines. Take them into your own hands as they are more important to you and your family than they are to anyone else. Know what the deadlines are for applications, how the process works for renting houses, even how the immigration process works. Mark all the deadlines in your calendar and/or reminders system to ensure that they are not missed.

When Evelyn moved to Switzerland, she and her husband went there on a familiarization and decision-making trip. They had a look at some houses and apartments that were within their budget so they could understand the type of housing they might be able to afford but thought they had plenty of time when they arrived to find the house they wanted. What they didn't know was that because of idiosyncrasies in the housing market in the Swiss canton to which they were moving, leases almost always end and begin on two days of the year. When they finally arrived, just after one of those two days, all that was left on the market were the places in which no one wanted to live. Lesson learned!

Priorities are often very personal, but for most people, the essentials of life in the new country are the highest priority. Priority lists often look like this.

- Housing/ moving stuff
- Schools
- Bank accounts
- Everything else

Many people breathe a huge sigh of relief when the first three are done, and take a more laissez-faire approach to everything else. But think carefully about the other items on the list. Letting them slide now may mean that they are much harder to complete once you are abroad, or that you never get back to them and expose yourself to significant risk or consequences in the future.

Do something every day

Moving internationally can mean that there's a huge amount to get done. It can even feel like a full-time job, and when it all needs to be juggled within the context of existing jobs and responsibilities at home, it can be hard to make any progress at all. On top of that, for many corporate moves, the bulk of the organization falls to the expat partner as the assignee is often expected to start travelling to the new location or even begin living and working there before the formal relocation date. Faced with the seemingly insurmountable, it is tempting to procrastinate, so to keep the momentum going and avoid feeling even more overwhelmed, make a habit of doing something every day.

Know what service providers are being paid to do for you

If your organization pays for service providers to help you with the relocation process, ensure that you know what they can and can't do for you. Expats often report contentious relationships with service providers. These tensions are often the function of mismatched expectations – the expat family expects that the service provider will do something it has not been contracted to do. Sometimes service providers can provide optional services but won't do so unless asked. By clarifying what the service provider will and won't do for you, you avoid this mismatch in expectations, you're able to get the greatest benefit from the service that is being paid for, and you can identify any gaps where you think you might need additional help.

Hire someone to do the things requiring specialist local knowledge

Most companies will provide visa services and destination services to help assignees and their families negotiate local bureaucracy, whether it's getting the right visas, negotiating leases or confirming school places. If your company doesn't provide this kind of help, it's worth hiring someone personally as these issues are best done by those who have local knowledge and/or language skills. Mistakes can be costly or can even jeopardize a move.

However, that doesn't mean you can abdicate all responsibility. These third parties will still need direction from you. It's important that you educate yourself on the basics of how the processes work so that you can communicate your needs clearly and let those working for you know what's important. In the story of Evelyn's move to Switzerland above, she *did* have a real estate agent helping her, but the agent assumed that Evelyn knew that moving dates were limited; Evelyn wasn't aware that limited moving days were a possibility so didn't ask.

Some issues are particularly important to understand:

- the process, requirements and timing for getting visas, including potential hold-ups or pitfalls in obtaining them;
- the process for renting accommodation;
- your rights and responsibilities as a tenant, particularly for any elements you are committed to financially;

- accessibility of different residential areas to schools, workplaces and community facilities;
- school admission processes and associated deadlines; and
- your responsibilities towards anyone who is working for you.

Of course, this is not a comprehensive list – it will be different depending on individual needs – but our rule of thumb is this: if it's important to you, learn the basics of how it will work in your new country.

Make the most of your familiarization trip

Most companies pay for their international assignees to make a trip to their future location to check out houses and schools and get a general impression of how life will be in the new country. Some companies allow couples or families to make a trip prior to making the decision to move, but the majority wait until the decision is made. By this time, the focus of the trip is largely practical, and as the story below demonstrates, it's important to be engaged in what it encompasses.

Jo Ryan and her family agreed to move to Shanghai with her husband's employer. The company engaged the services of a destination services provider in Shanghai to help them with school visits and the process of finding and securing a home. Having moved previously, Jo wisely asked her relocation consultant to send her a copy of the proposed itinerary in the week before they made their house-hunting trip. Thank goodness she did. The relocation consultant, keen to show off her city, had scheduled a day and a half of sightseeing at the beginning of the trip instead of allowing time to visit houses and schools more than one time if necessary. Had Jo and her husband stuck with the original schedule, they would not have had the time they needed to make those important decisions. In the end, they took the time necessary to get housing and schooling right and managed to squeeze in a few hours of sightseeing before heading home.

Selecting housing and schools are top of the list for families, but also consider visits for services that are important to you. For example, if you have a special medical need, make an appointment to visit any clinics or specialists on whom you will be relying. If your child has a particular sporting aptitude for which certain facilities are essential, make sure you visit them. Again, if it's important to you and your family, check it out.

Connect with people in your new country

One of the best sources of information to seek out in preparing for your move is people who already live there. They can help you to learn about your new environment and give you the inside track on where to live, what schools are good, how to get things done and whether there's anything you should bring from home that you won't be able to get after you move.

Don't know anyone in your new country and city? Start asking around. You'll be surprised by how many people know someone who knows someone. Colleagues may be able to introduce you to counterparts in your new country. Friends and family will almost always be delighted to introduce you to contacts they know who are living or have lived in your new country.

Once you have e-mail addresses and phone numbers, don't be shy about getting in touch. Expats are typically a helpful and friendly bunch. Most of them benefitted from the kindness of other expats when they moved, and most show their gratitude by 'paying it forward' – helping new arrivals. You'll have your chance to help another expat one day. Don't forget though that expats will give you their advice based on their own experiences, circumstances and preferences. Yours may be different, so talk to more than one person if you can and trust your own judgement.

Reflection time 6.0

How will you organize the preparation process?

What are the priorities and who will be responsible for starting to organize them?

Prepare yourself legally and financially

In Chapters Three and Four, we talked about understanding how moving abroad might affect your legal and financial positions. We can't emphasize how important it is to take care of these issues. Of course, what you need to put in place depends on where you come from, where you are moving to, who is in your family, and your circumstances. We can't give you information about every permutation, but here we share some legal and financial basics.

Legal

Wills, visas, work permits and professional registrations

Make sure you know what documentation you need in order to have the right to live and work or study in the country you are moving to. It is likely that you will be relying on a third party to obtain these documents on your behalf, but you should still have a basic understanding of the process. Certainly, you should know what you will be required to provide, what you need to do in order to obtain those documents and how long the process will take. For some countries, it may be a straightforward process with simple documentation requirements; for others you may need to provide additional documents. In our respective moves, we've had to provide police records, apostilles (certificates confirming the legality of official documents to other jurisdictions), medical test results, dozens of passport photos and more.

Caron Pope, Managing Partner of Fragomen Worldwide, the world's largest provider of immigration services, suggests that employee *and* partner have a high-level and very open conversation with their adviser at the beginning of the process so that any issues can be flushed out. She warns against asking someone else to provide personal information, as only you and your partner know your personal details in the detail and depth that is required.[54] According to Ms Pope, common pitfalls in the visa process include:

- getting clarity regarding your *legal* marital status – same-sex or cohabiting relationships are not universally recognized;
- obtaining visas for stepchildren;
- forgetting about previous criminal convictions (or not disclosing them to your partner);
- packing the documentation needed for an immigration application in your sea container where it can't be accessed;
- obtaining visas for domestic helpers or extended family members (adult children or parents); and
- assuming the partner will be able to work while abroad.

You need to be clear about the rights that your visa will confer, and understand the restrictions that apply.

Power of attorney

If you know you'll have financial or legal affairs to administer in your home country while you're living abroad, consider having a power of attorney drafted in favour of a trusted relative or your legal representative. This will give them the right to act on your behalf when you are unable to do so yourself. It can be made as specific or general as you need it to be.

Your rights as a couple

Your marriage or domestic arrangement may be recognized in your home country but could have a different legal standing, or might even be illegal, in your host country. You will have explored this in your decision-making process, but if you need to put additional provisions in place, this is when you should act.

If you have not already done so, this is also the time to understand what your respective rights will be regarding your ability to stay, your assets and custody if your relationship ends in divorce while you are living overseas.

This excerpt from an interview with Lucy Greenwood demonstrates the potential complexity when couples split up overseas and children are involved:

'Generally assume that the country in which the child is residing is their "habitual residence". If your relationship is falling apart, see a family lawyer in the country of their habitual residence before you do anything, even moving out of the family home in case you are not permitted to do so without the other parent's consent. If you are contemplating moving to another country, even if you deem that to be your 'home country', you certainly need to check what parental rights you both have as a consequence of your relationship status in the country in which you are residing. If you leave without one parent's permission you can in very many countries be committing civil and/or possibly criminal child abduction under the Hague Convention. (A list of those countries is shown at www.hcch.net/en/states/hcch-members) It can also be a criminal offence.

There can also be serious implications for your immigration status and care must be taken to check these issues before acting in too reactionary a manner.

Perhaps the countries where the ramifications can be most serious are non-Hague Convention countries, including those in the Middle East. In many Middle East countries Sharia laws apply (and Sharia law can often still be used by your partner even if you are both nationals of non-muslim countries). Also, if you are only able to remain in a country on your dependant's visa, in extreme cases, you could be forced to leave the country quickly, but possibly without your children!

Family law around the world is very different and its best to assume that the legal rights you or your partner have upon separation, in respect of children and financial rights, will be different in each and every country in which you reside. They even differ considerably between England and Scotland!'[55]

For financial matters, marital agreements (pre-nuptial agreements or post-nuptial agreements) can be useful. For children, written back-up plans (in case things don't go as you hope) can provide helpful evidence if disputes arise later. Of course, no one thinks that their marriage will end in divorce but Lucy recommends a consultation with a specialist international family lawyer, both in the country you are leaving and the one you are considering moving to, can be invaluable. Sadly, most couples fail to do so and wait instead until they separate, by which time their options might already have been compromised.

Wills

A valid will in your home country may not be enough. Your host country may not honour it, or may have a different approach to inheritance matters than your home country – so it's important that you also make a valid will in your host country.

Neil Long, a partner at UK law firm Bond Dickinson, suggests that couples should make wills in their host country, their home country and any other countries in which they own real property. He also notes the importance of making sure that your legal representatives in each country are aware of the other wills so that they can 'fit them together like a jigsaw' to ensure that nothing is missed and that the existence of one does not inadvertently invalidate the other. Sometimes families are reluctant to incur the expense of re-doing wills or having wills in different countries. However, the consequences of dying intestate in a foreign country, particularly where inheritance, tax, and guardianship laws differ from those in your home country, can be difficult for your heirs, both financially and emotionally. Moreover, it can, as Mr Long says, 'put a burden on the recently bereaved that they might not be ready to accept or have difficulty coping with'.[56]

Guardianship of children

Guardianship of children should be covered in your wills, but it is worth a specific mention. It is important not only to name guardians but also to ensure that if the guardians are delayed, you have nominated someone local to act *in loco parentis*. It is also worth finding out what, if anything, you need to do in the country you will be living in to ensure that anyone who is responsible for your children has *in loco parentis* if both you and your partner are outside the country.

Travelling alone with children

Not all countries will allow one parent to travel with their children without the permission of the other. If either you or your partner anticipates travelling alone with your children, ensure that you know what documentation is necessary.

Your voting rights

Make sure you understand if and how your voting rights change in your home country when you are resident in another country. If you retain voting rights in your home country, register for a postal vote if you can.

You may have help from your company or a relocation adviser on work and residence documents, but the other documents discussed above are rarely addressed by sponsoring organizations or relocation advisers. While this list is not comprehensive, it is intended to get you thinking about the legal documentation you need. To get a comprehensive view of the documentation required for your own circumstances, talk to legal advisers in both your home and host countries.

Financial

Managing your financial affairs remotely

As we discussed above, there may be issues, some of them financial, for which you will need to confer power of attorney. Set yourself up to manage all other issues remotely. Establish remote access to accounts through Internet and telephone banking, elect to receive statements and notices online and check that you have contact numbers for clients calling from abroad. If you have a mortgage payment or any bills that need to be paid regularly, set up direct debits if you don't already have them and ensure that the account from which they will be taken is regularly funded from your salary or another bank account.

Pensions and tax-advantaged investments in your home country

In your decision-making process, you should have learned how moving abroad would affect your ability to continue to contribute to public and private pension funds and how it might affect the magnitude of payments you receive in the future. Before you leave, you should also ensure that you complete and submit any documentation that is required to maintain your rights. Ensure you do this for both partners.

Preparing for financial dependence

Financial dependence can be a sticky issue. The emotional component to this dependency is not entirely separable from the financial one. A partner without a source of income may no longer have financial security. Couples deal with financial dependence in different ways. Some pool all their assets. Others choose to retain their separate assets prior to moving but put all subsequent earnings, savings and assets into joint accounts. Still others continue to keep everything separate. Some couples take the additional step of entering into a post-nup when one partner becomes financially dependent. Lucy Greenwood says that although these arrangements are not legally binding in many jurisdictions, they can help in some countries to demonstrate evidence of intent should the relationship turn sour.[57] It is also sensible to ensure that both partners have bank accounts in their sole names, so that should anything happen to one partner and access to joint assets is denied, there is still money that is accessible. Here are other practical ways to prepare for financial dependency.

- *Household expenses* – If you have previously split all household expenses, you will likely have to create a new arrangement for paying for them. We can't tell you what that arrangement should be, but it should account for the changed circumstances based on a budget that is agreed and reviewed regularly by both.
- *Personal expenses* – Personal expenses can be tricky in situations of financial dependence. Partners used to independent incomes may feel bad about spending money they are not earning. Partners earning the income may feel resentful if dependent partners overspend, or may take the attitude that 'it's my money so I can do what I want'. Consider setting an agreed budget for each partner and perhaps an agreed upper limit on individual expenditures, above which you must consult with each other before making the purchase.
- *Stay involved* – Many financially dependent partners abdicate responsibility for their household finances to their partners, leaving them to carry sole responsibility and putting themselves at risk in the event of death or divorce. Ensure you both have access to your accounts, you both participate in budget, expenditure and investment decisions, you both take ownership for your financial well-being and you both understand your overall financial position and health.
- *Access to money* – In some countries, if you have a dependent visa, you may not be able to have your own bank account or even be a joint owner with your partner on a bank account. Yet having to ask your partner for money for every need can be incredibly disempowering. If you or your partner will not be able to have a bank account, it's essential that you discuss how you will manage access to cash.

 Reflection time 6.1

What do you need to consider and prepare from a legal and financial perspective?

Prepare for your career move

In this part of the book, we'll discuss how assignees and partners who are continuing their careers while abroad can get the greatest benefit from their move. There are a few important practical preparations to consider at this stage.

Role objectives

Prior to leaving for your assignment, ensure that you have clarity regarding its objectives:

- What are the key performance indicators for your role?
- How will those be measured?
- Who will evaluate whether you have achieved them?

Important connections

Take time before leaving for your assignment to cement your relationships with key decision-makers at home. It will be much easier to continue to communicate once you are abroad if you have broken the ice before leaving.

Partners who want to find work abroad

Of course, you can leave this until you arrive in your new location, but in our opinion, it is always good to arrive with a plan and take action to initiate your career search on arrival.

- Consider what you can do now to initiate your job search process.
- Prepare your CV.
- Speak to local recruitment consultants in your new destination.
- Network through professional groups to find helpful connections.
- Ask your partner's organization if they provide career consultancy or recruitment support in situ.

Ask for a 'pre start'

In his book, *Foreigner in Charge*, Padraig O'Sullivan[58] recommends that, if possible, assignees agree a 'pre-start date' before the official start date. This is a period of ideally two weeks, during which time they can get to know their responsibilities and the people with whom they will be working before they officially take the role. During these first few weeks abroad they also support their partner and family. This way, expats are better equipped to make a strong start in the job and are not fully absorbed in the role until after their families have moved.

Reflection time 6.2

What initial steps do you need to take to support your career while you are abroad?

Prepare on behalf of others

Relocating with children

Moving abroad with children can be a complex and emotive undertaking. Whole books have been written on the subject. Our objective here is not to give you a comprehensive perspective on the issue but to get you thinking about the bigger questions.

Children's education

Deciding how to educate your children in an international environment can be tricky. Expats have more options than ever for their children's education. Overall that's a big positive. It means that in many (though not all) locations, families don't *have* to send their children to boarding school to maintain the quality of their education. But more choice can be confusing. Families can choose between local schools, bilingual schools, international schools (more and more of which are offering bilingual options) and boarding schools, all of which have different advantages and disadvantages. The decision-making process can be overwhelming, and parents often panic about making the wrong choice – after all, what is more important than your children's education?

The goal is to get your children into a school where they will thrive, one that is right for them and their individual needs. There is a whole host of factors to bear in mind. Here are some of the issues that we think are important to consider in making the choice.

- *The age of your children* – The implications of a tough adjustment are less disruptive for most younger children, so you may decide to trade off a more difficult transition in exchange for language and cultural benefits.
- *The personality of your children* – Some children will have a more difficult time adapting to a new school environment than others. As a parent, you will need to decide what is right for each child as well as the family overall.
- *Your children's educational goals* – What you want your children to get out of their education and what they want to accomplish themselves can be huge factors in choosing the right school. Needs for specific outcomes may make some schools more desirable than others.
- *Special needs* – If you have a child with special needs, find out what support is available *and at what cost* in the schools you are considering.

Special needs are handled differently in different systems, and the support your child requires might not be available or might come at a high price. Don't assume that an international school teaching your national curriculum will offer the same level of support you'd get at home.

- *The school systems on offer* – Understand the differences between the school systems you are considering. Go beyond the content of the curriculum and gain an understanding of the teaching philosophy, assessment method and progression through the system. Don't underestimate the challenge of changing between school systems.

When Evelyn and her husband moved from Shanghai to Michigan, their children moved from an English international school to an American local school. They reviewed the curricula with both schools to determine the school year into which their daughter would be enrolled (their son was only four). What no one really understood was that although the two curricula had a huge overlap, and of course there was no real language difference, teaching philosophies couldn't have been more different. On top of that, they did not understand that it was common practice for families to hold their children back in the school system. As a result, their daughter had a very difficult year both academically, in coming to grips with new ways of being taught, and socially, as she was almost two years younger than several of the students in her class.

- *Where you'll go next and when* – Families who, make one international move and either stay put or go home will often make different decisions than those who anticipate serial international relocations. Change has less impact if it is one-off or permanent, so serial expats who anticipate frequent change will often choose to sacrifice the language and cultural benefits of local schooling for the educational consistency offered by the international school system.
- *Whether your children will have input into the choice* – For older children, it may help their transition if they have a degree of ownership in the decision.
- *Whether your children will accompany you or not* – In some countries, you may not be able to meet your children's educational needs. If you can't, then boarding school is an option for many families.
- *Resources needed by your children who stay at home* – Whether you leave children behind in boarding school or in university, determine

what support they are going to need, and how and by whom that support will be delivered.

- *Your capacity to support your children through transition* – Changing schools and systems can be difficult and the more change you make, the more support your children are likely to need. It's therefore imperative that you consider your capacity to support that transition.

- *Your willingness to go out of your comfort zone* – Sending your children to a school whose system is different from the one in which you were educated or which teaches in a language you don't speak can be uncomfortable; your decision may be influenced by how involved you want to be in supporting your children's education. Remember though, it's about your children, not you.

- *School fees: how much and who's paying* – Last but not least, money can have a huge influence on what you choose. International schools can be as expensive as the top private schools in your home country. Your decision may well be influenced by the amount of support you receive from your sponsoring organization, your overall family finances and the number of years you anticipate having to pay.

If you feel overwhelmed by options for your children's education, or if you simply don't have time to do the research yourself, several resources, from websites to consultants, can help you make the right decision for your children. You'll find a list of resources at the end of the book.

Eldercare

If you are leaving elderly parents or other relatives behind, ensuring that they receive care when they are unable to care for themselves may be essential for your peace of mind and theirs. Even if siblings, friends or other relatives are able and willing to shoulder the responsibility in your absence, having a care plan can still be important. When it comes to ensuring the right care for elderly relatives, consider the following.

Care they currently need

Whether someone will be checking in with them daily or ensuring that they are comfortable and well looked after in residential care, or anything in between, it is much easier to put the care they need in place before you go. A first step is to have an honest conversation with your relatives to discuss what they might need in your absence.

Care they need in the future

A change in care needs for an elderly relative or an emergency can be a nightmare for an expat family. It may not be possible for you or your partner to drop everything and fly across continents to deal with a change or an emergency, much as you might want to. Care may also be needed sooner than you can get there. Regardless of how robust their health is now, have an agreed contingency plan with a qualified service provider who has the proper instructions and authority to act. This way, nothing falls between the cracks.

As Alison Hesketh of TimeFinders UK says, by having the conversation with your elderly relatives before you reach a crisis and by putting a contingency in place, you give yourself and your relatives the peace of mind that if they need more support in the future, it will be taken care of.[59]

Pets

Moving pets is not always possible or practical, but if you do decide to move them, you will probably need to engage specialist help to get them through 'pet immigration'. In any case, there's a lot to consider.

- *Do you want to take your pets with you?* Few people take small pets such as hamsters, rabbits, fish, etc. Taking larger domestic animals may not be possible due to their age or health.
- *If you don't want to take them, what do you need to do to rehome them?* Can a relative or friend adopt your pet or will you have to consider other alternatives?
- *If you do want to take them, will they be allowed into your host country and how will you make it happen?* What documentation will you need? Do they need medical checks or vaccinations? Will you be required to quarantine them when they arrive and if so, where and for how long?
- *How will they travel?* Will they travel with you? If not, who will drop them off/pick them up? Do you need a special carrier for them to travel in? Will they need to be sedated?
- *How much will it cost and who will pay for it?* Moving a pet overseas is expensive, so it's important to understand how much the move will cost and whether your company will pay for it.
- *Will you be able to bring your pet home again?* It may be possible to move your pet to your new country, but coming home may not be so easy. What will you have to do to bring your pet home again?

Reflection time 6.3

*What action do you need to take to prepare for your children's educational needs,
the care of elderly relatives and the management of any pets?*

Prepare for a soft landing

Much of what we discussed earlier in the chapter *must* get done, but you can
do a few things to simply give yourself some breathing space when you arrive.

Start building your network

Make personal and professional connections with people already living in your
new city and country. Find out what organizations can help you to meet people
and start building your networks. Ask your company to provide connections or
perhaps a local mentor to help you through the early days.

Make regular appointments

If you visit the doctor, dentist or hairdresser on a regular basis, schedule those
visits at home as close to your departure as possible so that when you arrive,
you have some time to find the right services for you.

Prepare to get up and running fast

When you arrive in a new country, you will want to get your personal and
administrative life up and running as quickly as possible. Our many moves
have taught us that careful preparation can make the difference between functioning and frustration. Here are the actions we suggest to help you get there.

- Set aside important documents and hand-carry them – particularly those needed to navigate officialdom in your new country (save
  scanned copies too).
- Put all your personal data files onto a cloud-based storage system such
  as Dropbox and back them up.
- If you know where you're going to live, change your address with everyone who needs to know. If you can't do that, subscribe to a mail-for-
  warding service.
- Plan to purchase a pay as you go SIM card for your phone and a data
  SIM for your tablet or computer as soon as you arrive so that you can
  communicate as quickly as possible.
- If you can, open and fund a bank account in your new country before
  you arrive. If you can't, ensure you have access to cash.

- Work out the location of key places relative to your home to increase your confidence when you need to visit them (include accident and emergency services in this list; we can both vouch for the fact that there are few things more stressful than trying to locate A&E in a foreign city when someone is bleeding).

Plan some downtime when you arrive

If you can, book some time off for your first few days 'in country'. It's much more fun and less stressful to get to know a city with your partner and family; plus you'll probably be in need of a break to recover from the move. Plan to be at home any time the movers are around too – it's easier if you have two people directing removal traffic.

 Reflection time 6.4

What can you do now to give yourself breathing space when you arrive?

Summary

❑ The practical preparation for an international move is like an extra full-time job, but doing it well can help you to get off to a great start in your new country and give you time to focus on the emotional aspects of leaving your home country. There are five broad categories of effective preparation:
   - creating a system that gets you through the overwhelming logistics of the physical move;
   - ensuring that you are financially and legally prepared for your life abroad;
   - getting the support structure in place that will help your career to flourish overseas;
   - getting the right educational and eldercare resources in place so your dependents are taken care of and you have peace of mind; and
   - taking actions now that will make your first few weeks in your new country less stressful.

CHAPTER SEVEN

Preparing for the emotions of moving

'When you move from one country to another you have to accept that
there are some things that are better and some things that are worse,
and there's nothing you can do about it.'
Bill Bryson

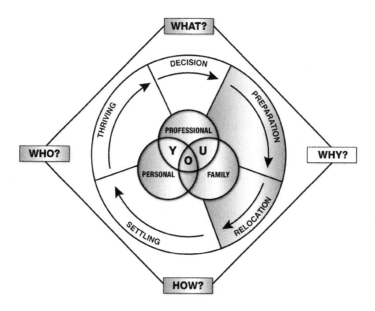

Jenny and Paul

Paul's conversation with Jean was enjoyable. It was good to feel that his experience and insights could help smooth the relocation process for someone else. The conversation made him realize how much he had learned through the relocation experience. It had been developmental in many ways. Jean seemed appreciative, and while she was interested to learn about his job search, she was more concerned about the challenges of relocating her children. Her two teenagers had two very different reactions to the move. One was excited; the other was apprehensive and angry at the prospect of leaving friends she loved. Paul could relate to this. He had been sad to leave his colleagues but as an adult could rationalize these feelings. He could see how a young teenager might struggle. James, his son, had been heartbroken as he said goodbye to his friends and grandparents. It had been tough to watch. But it had been important to say their goodbyes properly. No point pretending it was anything different. They had promised him that they would all connect through Skype, and made a point of establishing regular chat times with his grandparents and best friend. That had helped, but there was no doubt it took time to adjust. The new school had been great at helping him to integrate and build new friendships. Paul had made a big effort to invite new friends home and get to know other parents – not an easy feat as one of the only male parents regularly at the school gates. But this was one good thing about an international school: everyone understood from personal experience the challenges involved. From an emotional perspective, there was no doubt relocation could be a rocky ride. But love, support and patience all helped... and time. Adjustment took time. There was no magic solution.

Practical preparation is essential; after all, you need somewhere to live, boxes have to be packed, paperwork must be put in order. For many, practical preparation is so all-consuming that emotional considerations are pushed to the back of their minds. Jean is right to be thinking about her children's reactions. Adding more to your metres-long to-do list might seem unnecessary and stressful, but preparing yourself and your family members for the emotional impact of moving can make a tremendous difference to your experience in the first few weeks or even months of your new life. And it's not just about your early experience; there are far-reaching implications too. A difficult transition can affect your mindset and resilience well beyond the move, making it more challenging to have a positive and affirming experience.

In this chapter, we look at the two distinct emotional phases of moving overseas:

- the emotions related to leaving; and
- the emotions related to the transition to your new life.

'Awareness is like the sun. When it shines on things they are
transformed.'
Thich Nhat Hanh

Of course, being aware of the challenges that might be ahead won't totally insulate you from their effects, but at least they won't surprise you, and you'll be in a better position to successfully navigate them.

The real key to getting through hard parts is action. There are some proactive strategies you can employ as a family and as individuals to help you to deal with the emotional aspects of moving to another country. Some of those strategies are built around understanding and supporting each other; others involve practical steps you can take to limit the impact of certain issues. In this chapter, we discuss each issue, explain its potential impact and outline the strategies that you and your family members can put in place to help make your transition as smooth as possible.

Relocation: a life-changing event

Change is all about the transition from one state to another. By relocating internationally you are altering your:

- living environment;
- professional environment;
- culture and language; and
- social life, relationships, networks and connections.

Everything in your daily life is about to change. The context of your life will take on a completely new form. While change is exciting and associated with many opportunities and potential benefits, it can be an uncomfortable ride at times. You may encounter personal resistance, as Jean did. You might be happy and full of anticipation one day, sad the next. Stress will not help this roller coaster of emotions. It is important as you prepare that you build time into your daily routines to relax, sleep, eat healthily and spend time together, without the list! Talk about the move and listen to each other's thoughts, both positive and negative.

Leaving

'Before you begin something new, you have to end what used to be....
So beginnings depend on endings, the problem is, people don't like
endings.'
William Bridges

It is tempting to pack and run. To say, 'We'll be back soon' and avoid the pain of saying goodbye. But to do this is to run from the truth, which is that this move represents the end of one phase of your life. You will never return to everything as it now is. Louise knows this only too well, having repatriated twice in her international journey. Life moves on, you change and your friends and family also change. This is not a bad thing, but it's important to recognize that while you can go 'back' geographically, you can never go 'back' to life completely as it was. It is important to make time to say goodbye.

Work with third culture kids (TCKs), children who have spent a portion of their formative years (0–18) in a culture different from that of their parents, has identified the sense of loss these goodbyes can create and the challenges that can arise if this loss is not acknowledged. Unresolved grief can lead to psychological challenges such as denial, anger, depression, withdrawal from relationships and rebellion later in life.[60]

This underlines the importance of taking time to acknowledge the sadness and loss involved in leaving. As the William Bridges quote above illustrates, it's difficult to move on until you've processed what it means to you. And it's not just about you. If you have children, a focus on only the positives of your move may send a silent signal to them that it's not OK to feel sad.

Before you relocate, take time to think about how you will leave in terms of saying goodbye. It can be tempting to slip away quietly and avoid any emotional goodbyes, but this can have negative implications for both yourself and those you leave behind. We know from experience how important it is to acknowledge and celebrate the relationships that you value.

Part of this process is the sense of assurance you give to friends and family that they are still important to you; reassuring them that although you will be further apart geographically, you still want them to play an important part in your life.

And yes, it can be the last thing you want to think about from an organizational perspective. Arranging meet-ups and social events to say goodbye can be one event too many when you are already up to your ears with the planning and preparation for your move. It can also be emotional for everyone concerned – some goodbyes are straightforward, others can be overwhelming.

Evelyn usually copes with saying her farewells to her friends, but there is something about watching her children say goodbye to school and teachers that leaves her a sobbing mess. Also, different people react in different ways. One person may appear to manage well at the time only to break down at the slightest provocation a few days later. Another may be extremely emotional at the point of saying goodbye but recover the following day and never mention it again. This is the time to be sensitive to individual ways of coping and to provide a listening ear and a shoulder to cry on when required.

Ruth van Reken and David Pollock[61] also say that it is important not only to acknowledge and say goodbye to people, but also to pets, possessions and places that have played a significant part in your life. All these goodbyes mark the end of one experience and bring closure ahead of a new beginning.

> *When Louise and her family left the island of Madeira in Portugal, they held a big party for their daughters, who were then four and seven. It would have been easier not to bother as there was so much to do before leaving. However, they realized it was important to celebrate their friends and the time they had all spent together. Now they have a photo album packed with happy memories of that day with their friends, many of whom remain good friends years later.*

Think destination

Remember however, that acknowledging and saying goodbye does not mean that once abroad you will not think back to your old home and feel sadness for what you have left behind, for your friendships and relationships there. We might label this feeling homesickness and perhaps a sense of longing for what once was.

To balance out the potential sadness it is helpful to think forward to the future and your new destination. Excitement may form part of the picture; remember also to prepare yourself for day-to-day reality when you arrive. Much of this book has been about exactly that; understanding the potential opportunities and challenges, making plans and creating strategies that will give you the best start for your new life abroad.

Reflection time 7.0

How will you prepare to leave? How will you say goodbye to friends and family?

Preparing for the adjustment to your new life

Life in a new country and culture is fascinating and exciting but the adjustment can be emotionally difficult. You may experience adjustment in almost every aspect of your life: personal, professional and social. As we discussed above, the point of this chapter is creating awareness of the emotionally challenging aspects of relocation.

In his book *Safe Passage*, Doug Ota talks about the importance of social attachments and the brain's response to their absence.[62] He argues that moving activates an 'alarm system' in the brain that prevents people from focusing on higher-order functions such as self-development until they have secure social attachments in place. Teenagers, who are loosening their attachments to parents and creating stronger peer attachments, can be particularly affected by moving, but the principle also applies to younger children and adults alike. It also explains why transition is often easier for assignees – they have continuity in a work culture that is at least somewhat familiar.

Adjustment to a new culture

One factor impacting your personal, professional and social adjustment is cultural adjustment. Before we discuss cultural adjustment in more detail, it's useful to define 'culture'. It turns out it's not so simple; academics struggle to agree on what culture is. We've read dozens of definitions of the word, and the one which seems to provide the best foundation for a discussion on cultural adjustment was coined by Helen Spencer-Oatey:

> '...a fuzzy set of basic assumptions and values, orientations to life, beliefs, policies, procedures and behavioural conventions that are shared by a group of people, and that influence (but do not determine) each member's behaviour and his/her interpretations of the "meaning" of other people's behaviour.'[63]

With this definition, it's easy to see why culture is such a pervasive theme in the adjustment process. You will experience the impact of culture in different situations as you relocate. There will be the new national culture, and for the assignee, a new work culture. For the family, there will be a new educational culture, and for everyone, new social networks and cultures associated with those. A starting point for understanding new cultural perspectives is to understand your own cultural blueprint in terms of your personal assumptions, values, beliefs and behaviours.

In terms of adjustment, you may be familiar with the term 'culture shock', which is used to describe the emotional reaction to operating in another culture. It was first defined by Kalervo Oberg in a seminar at the Women's Club of Rio de Janeiro in 1954[64] and has been widely research, analysed and discussed since. The word 'shock' implies that it will be experienced suddenly and disappear suddenly, but it's a process. The graph below provides a pictorial representation of the *process* of adjusting to a new culture. That's why we prefer to talk about cultural adjustment rather than culture shock. There are several distinct phases to the process.

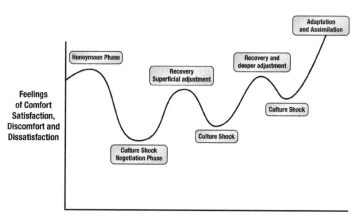

Phases of Adjustment to Change and Cultural Environment

In the *honeymoon phase*, everything is new and exciting. You enjoy the novelty of new experiences and embrace the differences.

During *the negotiation phase*, the differences start to seem less charming. You become frustrated because you don't know how to get things done, everything takes longer and you don't understand language and social cues. It's a time when you may experience more downs than ups, and can be characterized by frustration, anger, anxiousness and feelings of isolation and helplessness. There may be a feeling that expectations don't match reality, and a resulting need to compromise.

In the *recovery phase*, you start to feel more confident and competent in your day-to-day life; the ups start to outnumber the downs. You feel more positive about your life and more able to cope with challenges. This phase may include a period of *superficial adjustment*, where you have adjusted to the surface level of the culture but have not got to grips with the more subtle aspects. A few more dips may occur as you react to more novel situations and challenges. These are often then followed by a deeper level of adjustment and recovery.

Finally, you reach *the adaptation and assimilation phase*, where you begin to feel integrated into the culture and are able to navigate it with fluency.

You'll notice the graph looks like a wave – you may go through the cycle several times. The ups and downs may be less severe each time, working towards deeper adjustment as you learn about your new culture and adapt your behaviour to it.

Everyone is different

We intentionally haven't put time frames on any of these phases. This is because *everyone experiences the process differently*. If you're still feeling angry and frustrated after six months and your spouse is sailing through life, that doesn't mean you're not adapting – it just means it's taking longer or that you are at different stages, experiencing different emotions at different times. Not everyone goes through these phases. Some may experience a small dip and nothing more. The important point is to be aware and therefore prepared.

It doesn't matter where you go

Everyone expects to experience culture shock moving to a vastly different culture, and underestimates it in countries with common language or roots. But don't be fooled. Cultural differences are everywhere. George Bernard Shaw once described the US and the UK as 'two countries separated by a common language'. In fact, the less you expect cultural differences, the more difficult you may find dealing with them.

It's not over until it's over

Over time, you'll likely find the ups and downs of adjustment decrease in amplitude, and you'll feel more at ease with life. But that doesn't mean that there won't be days or even weeks where you feel frustrated by the differences. Sometimes these experiences will be a function of what you are doing; trying something new perhaps. Other times they will be a function of how you feel; perhaps a task has not gone the way you expected. When Evelyn lived in Shanghai, expats referred to good days and bad days as 'Shang-highs' and 'Shang-lows'.

Navigating cultural adjustment

Coming to grips with cultural adjustment takes time, but here are a few things you can do to help manage the process.

- *Remember, it's not wrong, it's different.* Your own culture is deeply ingrained in the way you behave and react. You may only be aware of how it affects you when your host and home culture conflict and you experience an almost visceral reaction. We've both learned that reminding yourself of the mantra 'it's not wrong, it's different' before you respond can help you form a more productive response and lessen your reaction over time.

- *Understand the cycle.* Knowing that it's normal won't make it go away, but you won't have to deal with the added stress of personalizing the experience and thinking that it's just you who's going through it. Be aware also that transition has its own energetic and cognitive cost that is often underestimated.

- *Communicate and support each other.* Talk about your experiences with your partner and family so that your loved ones understand where you are in the process and what you're going through. And cut them some slack if you know that their behavior might be a function of where they are in the process.

- *Learn about the culture you're living in.* Being aware of how a culture differs from your own won't mean you'll avoid the process of adapting but it might make it less personal. It's easier to accept differences if you understand why they are what they are, and you're less likely to make embarrassing and confidence-eroding mistakes if you know your way around the culture. There are many ways to learn about cultural differences. Books and websites are often a good starting point and can give you basic information about the culture you are living in. If your company gives you the opportunity to participate in language and cross-cultural training, jump at the chance as it can get you off to a great start in understanding how to operate in your new culture.

- *Find friends in the shared experience.* The term 'expat bubble' often carries negative connotations; it describes expats who only socialize with other expats and never experience local life and culture. But the expat bubble can also provide essential support and relief. In the context of cultural adjustment, the bubble can be invaluable. Some experiences will make you cry, some may even test your sense of who you are. Your friends in the bubble, who share your experience, can laugh with you and help lift the burden.

- *Get help if you need it.* Most people eventually adapt, but some people get stuck in a rut and feel unable to move beyond the lows. In that case, it may be a sign of a deeper issue. If you feel that you are unable to lift yourself from the lows or you are concerned about a family member or friend, seek professional help or encourage your loved one to do so.

 Reflection time 7.1

What can you do to better understand the culture of the country you are relocating to?

What strategies can you begin to put in place to support you through the transition process and minimize the impact of culture shock?

Different roles, different challenges

While cultural adjustment is pervasive throughout every aspect of your new life, it is not the whole story. You will make many more adjustments in your professional, personal and social life. Each family member might face specific challenges in adapting to life in the new country. This section addresses each of those and suggests practical strategies for overcoming them. Of course, these challenges are not the exclusive domain of each individual. For example, an expat partner who is able or chooses to continue their professional life will likely experience the same workplace challenges as an assignee. Likewise, assignees need to build new social lives for themselves and may experience the same challenges as expat partners in that respect. We've addressed the issues in the context where they are likely to be experienced most acutely.

Assignees

While we talked about the benefit of a somewhat continuous social structure for assignees earlier in the chapter, assignees may go through several different types of transition in relation to the workplace and family. As an assignee, you are often moving into a new role and reporting to a new leader while working in a new country. You are also dealing with the transition of the family to a new country and perhaps to new roles within your family. With six or seven transitions happening simultaneously, it's not surprising that some assignees struggle at first.

Adjusting to a new work culture

Branches of the same organization have their own cultures, so even if you remain in the same organization, you may find differences in organizational culture between home and host offices. Adjusting to this new culture may be just as challenging as adjusting to a new national culture; and potentially, more is at stake as mistakes can have a lasting effect on your ability to be effective. Even if one of your tasks in your job is to change the culture, it's important to understand it. Learning about the national culture can help you avoid major faux pas. It can also be invaluable to identify a trusted individual in your organization to help you navigate the cultural aspects of dealing with colleagues and customers. In a Thriving Abroad podcast interview, Jacquie Kane shared how she worked to understand her team in China – the cultural exchange process can be a two-way street.

'I read lots of books about business culture in China; I learned from Chinese co-workers, forming relationships with them to better understand the culture. They wanted to understand my culture and I dispelled some misperceptions. For example, some were surprised that I was working because they thought that for Westerners it was the men who worked and the women just stayed at home and painted their nails and watched TV all day.'

Adjusting to a new role

Beyond adapting to a new work culture, you may be adapting to a new role. While your new role may draw on skills and experiences you already have, it may also require that you develop new skills, do tasks in different ways and take on new leadership responsibilities. Being clear about what is expected of you and how your performance will be evaluated is key to knowing how to adapt to your new role. Identifying up front any additional support you might need to be successful is also important. Remember Padraig O'Sullivan's advice: negotiate a 'pre-start' so you can get to grips with your new culture, team and responsibilities before your 'official' start date in your new role.

Feeling torn between work and family demands

Like Jenny, when you move for a new role, you may find you have an overwhelming amount of work to do. This is particularly true if you are stepping into a role that requires extensive travel and entertaining, or requires you to determine and implement significant change. You might find that your work consumes most of your waking hours and you have little time for anything else.

This may leave you feeling torn between the demands of your family and the demands of your job. It can make you feel as if you are never in the right place and can be detrimental to both your productivity and your well-being.

Having frank conversations with your family about the demands of your job and how they may affect your ability to support them is important, but it's equally critical that you put boundaries around your work life so that you can carve out time for yourself and your family that doesn't involve work-related interruptions.

Expat partners

Being an expat partner is, perhaps, the biggest challenge of all, particularly if you've put your career on hold to move. You will have almost no continuity in any aspect of your life, and identity loss can be a significant issue. We talk more about this issue in Chapter Ten.

Dealing with financial dependence

For expat partners who do put careers on hold, one of the biggest adjustments they may experience is becoming financially dependent. It's not an issue to be taken lightly, and if not addressed, it can pose fundamental challenges to your relationship.

Financial dependence can have profound effects on behaviour and the balance of power within a relationship. In the previous chapter, we suggested that you talk to a financial adviser about some of the big-picture changes you might make to ensure that the financially dependent partner is protected and that your assets and liabilities are held in a way that makes you both comfortable. We believe that it is crucial for couples to discuss the personal impact of relocation and the consequential change on the dynamics of their relationship. Here are two issues we think are important for you to discuss:

- *Value each other's roles*; it can be easy to fall into a 'grass is greener', mentality with each partner viewing the other's role as the easy route. But when there is such an imbalance, it's fundamental that both partners acknowledge and value the contribution that the other makes to the family and the relationship. Like Jenny and Paul, it is important to give each other the space to express frustration about your new roles – being the sole breadwinner can bring extra stress and pressure, and not having a job or an income doesn't mean that you are leading a life of leisure.
- *In a relationship, money can equate to power*; nowhere is this more evident than in situations of financial dependence. It's important that you find a way to manage your money to maintain the balance of power in your relationship and that you both commit to open and honest dialogue about money. The following are common ways we have seen money alter the balance in a relationship.

- Money is labelled 'mine' and 'yours'.
- The financially dependent partner has to ask for money.
- The earning partner makes all the financial decisions and/or the dependent partner abdicates financial management to the earning partner.
- Either partner overspends the agreed budget.

Feeling overwhelmed by more logistics

The logistics of an international move don't end when you get on a plane. Everything needs to be unpacked and organized, services need to be connected, paperwork needs to be dealt with. And that's only the beginning. Everything is new, everything needs to be started from scratch and everything takes twice as long to do than it would at home. For a while, you may feel as if all you do is run errands or wait in your house for services to show up. It's important that you find a balance between getting things done in an acceptable time frame and giving yourself permission to begin building your new life. Make sure you schedule regular time to build a social network and pursue your own goals and objectives.

Creating a social network

When you move to a new country, you leave behind all your usual support systems, your partner is probably consumed by the new job and your children are at school all day. You may find yourself feeling isolated. You may not know anyone in your new community and it may be difficult to talk to your friends and family at home about your feelings as they probably won't understand what you are going through. It's important to carve out time to start building a social network for yourself, both from a practical perspective (to learn about your new life) and an emotional one (to make contacts who understand what you are going through). It can be nerve-wracking to go to new places where you don't know a soul, but expats are a friendly bunch. They've all been where you are and they will generally welcome newcomers.

 ### Reflection time 7.2

What challenges do you think may be an issue for you?

What strategies can you put in place to minimize their impact?

Children

Children experience the transition of moving countries differently. Numerous factors will affect their transition. Age is one of the most important factors, but personality will also be a contributor. We know people who, like Jean, have found that one child embraces their new life abroad and sails through the transition while the other finds the process extremely challenging.

Babies and toddlers

Very young children tend to be adaptable. They are most strongly attached to their parents; so long as they are with their parents, their transition period is likely to be relatively short. However, they may be unsettled by the lack of familiar objects around them or by unfamiliar food or climate. Toddlers may also miss other carers who had a significant role in their lives. They may also worry that they won't get to see these people again.

Make sure that you take comfort objects and toys with you in your air shipment or carry them with you. Keep as much continuity as possible for your younger children. They will soon adapt to the environment. Keep them connected with grandparents and family back home by asking loved ones to record videos of bedtime stories, and Skype or FaceTime when you can, even if your toddler only wants to talk for a minute or two.

Young children and tweens

This age group is also quite adaptable, although there is usually a period of transition as they start school and try to make friends and slot in. Compared with their younger siblings, they often have deeper attachments with a wider group of people, including extended family, teachers and friends. Try to keep those connections going to demonstrate that relationships continue despite geographical distance. You may also find that children this age do not fully comprehend the reality of moving until they are living abroad, and may experience a delayed reaction. When Evelyn's family moved from the US to Belgium, her son, then seven, had no problem with the move until his first day at his new school. It seemed that in starting school, the realization dawned on him that it wasn't a holiday and he wouldn't be going back to his old life. Children this age may surprise you by taking things you'd find difficult in their stride but reacting emotionally to the most unexpected events. You can help prepare them by talking to them about and showing them pictures of their new country and school. There are some excellent books that you can read with your children that will help them to understand and relate to the process. The film *Inside Out* is also a great resource. We have listed more resources in the children's section of the resource section of this book.

Teens

Moving with teens can be challenging, particularly if they have not had a say in the move or if you have asked their opinion but have gone against their wishes. Developmentally, teens are busy separating from their parents and forming strong attachments to friends and perhaps other adults, such as teachers. You, their parents, are taking them away from those important attachments, and you may become the focal point for all their pain and anger about the move. They may express that anger loudly and often, or they might withdraw completely. It's important that you allow them to express their feelings if they want to, even if it's uncomfortable or upsetting for you. Smartphones and myriad apps have made it simple for teens to communicate with friends and family at home, but it's important that they find a balance between the life they have left behind and their new life abroad. This is also an age where deeper problems can emerge. Look out for signs such as:

- sleep issues: either not sleeping or never getting out of bed;
- lack of appetite;
- lack of communication and engagement at home and/or school;
- unwillingness to interact with other students and their schoolwork;
- unusual behaviour, anger or aggression; and
- excessive connection to friends at home at the expense of creating new friends abroad.

This list is not exhaustive. Of course, there is likely to be a settling-in period and some reaction to the change. But, you know your child. If you're worried and feel your child is struggling more than they should, seek professional help.

Children who don't accompany you

Some parents choose to send their children to boarding school for education or security reasons. Other children remain in their home country for university or work. In either case, it can be challenging for both parents and children to manage the relationship across long distances. It's much easier with modern communications to stay in touch, but it's important that you create age-appropriate communication habits and structures to enable you to stay connected with each other's lives. Children in boarding school need a guardian, but arranging a trusted in-country contact even for older children will give both you and your children peace of mind.

 Reflection time 7.3

What strategies can you put in place to support your children?

Summary

❏ The emotional aspects of relocation are complex, but if ignored, they can have lasting effects on your well-being and on the well-being of your family.

❑ Take time to ensure that you leave well.

❑ Understand the potential impact of culture shock and be prepared to cope with the negative emotional fallout, both your own and your family members'.

❑ Recognize the impact of different roles and challenges on the adjustment process. Give yourself time to adjust.

❑ Consider how you aim to manage the challenge of financial dependency. Develop an approach that will work for both partners.

❑ Be aware that different children may respond to relocation in different ways. Look for signs of discomfort and offer a supportive, listening ear.

PART THREE

Arriving to Thriving Abroad

CHAPTER EIGHT

Unpacked but not settled – riding the waves of change

'We immediately become more effective when we decide to change
ourselves rather than asking
things to change for us.'
Stephen Covey

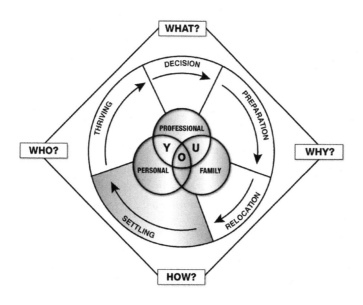

Rich and Angela

Two years in, Angela was thriving in her new life in London. She had a great job and loved the charm and frenetic pace of London. How things had changed since those first few tentative weeks and months. The first weeks in London had been an explosion of new experiences as they toured around London, sightseeing and enjoying the vibrant city atmosphere. Rich took a week's holiday to settle in, and they made use of every minute, getting to know the city and building new routines. Then, all too soon, Rich started work and Angela was left home with the IKEA flat packs and the mountain of boxes to sort. Suddenly the days seemed very long, particularly when Rich's work took him abroad. Angela launched herself on a familiarization project, visiting shops, museums and parks. However, walking the streets alone was not so much fun. This was the UK – she had thought she would just slot into this English-speaking country and had expected people to be friendly and open, like back home. But the British reserve and anonymity of London hit her hard. Angela found her old work pressures were replaced by a different kind of pressure; difficult to define but featuring an underlying sense of loneliness. This was something she resolved to keep to herself. Rich was finding his new role stressful and she didn't want to add to his load. Everything she set out to do seemed to be a challenge. She missed her old routine, friends, even her job. Rich noticed after a time that Angela was not her usual effervescent self. He suggested she look for a job. She had worked in the hospitality industry in the US and so started approaching hotels and restaurants. But they wanted her to be available for long shifts and weekends, and that would impact on the one current high of her life, the weekend travel to Europe. It's not that they went every weekend, but she was keen to realize that part of their dream. Angela had recognized she needed to work something out. The experience had to work for both of them, after all. Unclear how to move things forward by herself Angela had found a career consultant who helped her to define what she wanted to do and launch a targeted job search campaign.

Angela's story describes a typical picture of the mix of emotions, the highs and lows that can occur in the early days as you adjust to a new lifestyle abroad. The optimistic start, the excitement of the new beginning – these things don't continue forever. The reality of work commitments and settling-in challenges kicks in at some point. However capable you are, it takes time to integrate into the new environment and culture, both at work and at home.

The culture shock model described in Chapter Seven talks about the honeymoon period of anticipation, excitement and enthusiasm. This can be followed by a period of negotiation. William Bridges, in his book *Managing Transitions*, describes this time as the 'neutral zone': 'This psychological no-man's land, between the old reality and the new one.'[65]

While the physical relocation has a finite timeline – the boxes *will* all eventually be empty, the admin sorted – the timeline of the emotional transition isn't as concrete. On bad or sad days, you may find yourself questioning your decision to relocate in the first place. This is when the foundations laid in the decision and preparation stage will be invaluable. Reminding yourself of the purpose of your relocation and the opportunities that attracted you will help you to work through the potentially unsettling nature of this period.

As we saw in Chapter Seven, there is no right or wrong when it comes to people's reactions to change. Judge where you are personally in the process and be ready to support family members. Use the strategies contained in this chapter to support your personal change and settling-in process.

If you are struggling, remember, you don't need to do this alone. This book, the resources provided by Thriving Abroad and the support provided by your organization will help you to negotiate the transition stage and find your place and space in your new environment.

You have come a long way from the initial discussions about international relocation to living the experience. You have worked through considerable change and transition. As we start Part Three of the book, it's time to take stock and recognize your progress and achievements so far.

 Reflection time 8.0

Complete the exercise in the workbook on taking stock.

Understanding the three ways that adjustment impacts on you

Adjustment affects the way we think, feel and behave.[66]

Adjustment in the way you *think*: cognitive adjustment

Your thinking will change and develop as you acquire new knowledge about your host culture, organization and general environment. You will develop this knowledge in different ways: through internal thought processes, as you observe and recognize where your knowledge is sufficient or lacking, and through external sources, such as verbal and behavioral cues.[67]

Not everything about the new culture or way of operating in the general or work environment will be compatible with your old ways of thinking. You will need to adjust, or live with the inconsistencies and ambiguities.

While it is important to feel confident about your capability to operate effectively in the new cultural environment, it is useful to recognize what you don't know or understand.

The degree of challenge will also be mediated by the distance of the host culture from your home culture in terms of fundamental beliefs, values and cultural dimensions, and any previous experience you may have had in working cross-culturally and living in a different environment. If, as in the case of Angela, you have never had much need to develop your understanding of a different cultural perspective, it can be challenging to work out how to best integrate into the new culture.

Adjustment in the way you *feel*: emotional adjustment

We've talked about the rollercoaster ride of emotional highs and lows. Issues such as getting lost and arriving late, being the only newbie at social events and receiving less-than-helpful responses to your brave attempts to speak the new language can lead to disproportionate emotional reactions. Recognizing these feelings and understanding that they relate to the whole challenge of transition is part of the solution.

There is a lot to process, and the resulting cognitive and emotional challenge can mean that it is difficult to focus and follow through on goals. You may find yourself procrastinating and feeling frustrated by your lack of progress; you may criticise your new environment, the team at work and the local customs and ways of doing things. You may feel pessimistic about your experience, and begin to question whether you made the right choice.

At times, you may feel overly anxious, overwhelmed and stressed. While stress in moderation can be positive, prolonged stress can negatively affect your health and your cognitive performance.

Some of these symptoms of discomfort relate to the adjustment process, gaining new knowledge and developing new relevant competencies and skills. To explain, think about how you learn a new sport. As you upskill, perhaps during a training session, you learn new techniques and become very conscious of how you are playing. Often you will experience a dip in your performance as you work on the new skill; you may feel frustrated, even annoyed at yourself. Over time and with practice, that skill becomes integrated into your play and you no longer need to think consciously about it. This is similar to your experience now as you learn about your new environment and integrate new cultural knowledge and skills into your behaviour. Over time it will become the new normal. Just now it feels a bit clunky. The message here is, be prepared for some emotional reactions that seem out of proportion to the challenge or issue at hand.

Adjustment in the way you *behave*: behavioural adjustment

You may find that you need to adjust your behaviour to meet the local expectations and cultural norms. This can feel uncomfortable to begin with. It may show up in obvious ways, such as how you need to dress, greet people and conduct yourself in social settings.

As with Angela, you will need to find ways to build new social relationships, and this can be challenging when people don't react in the way you expect them to.

Loneliness and isolation are some of the challenges that people report in the early days abroad. Social connectedness is key to people's performance in life. Evidence suggests that loneliness induces the same threat response as pain, thirst and hunger; it can impact on our health and cognitive functioning. Increased social connection reduces the sense of threat and helps people to think and operate better and at a higher level; to see novel situations and perspectives. The opportunity to share thoughts and ideas helps people to learn quickly and apply that knowledge more effectively

Developing your way of thinking, and of managing emotional reactions and new capabilities, is all part of adjusting to the new context or environment.

The challenge is that while the novel activities in our lives can be positive and lead to learning and development, they can also lead to a sense of anxiety, defensiveness and even fear.

These feelings can mean that our fight or flight responses are triggered. Of course, we don't literally run away or stay and get our fists out (we hope). But we do take part in modern-day equivalents.

Our flight might involve making excuses, staying home and avoiding the challenges – and we have known people who have done that. In this way, we manage to evade the perceived embarrassment, but equally we learn nothing and become lonely in the process.

In fight mode, we might feel anger or frustration at our situation. We become victims and blame others – our partner, the company or even the country and its culture – for our discomfort. Our default behaviour becomes negative, disparaging and defensive; not a good place to be at all.

Fortunately, we can develop strategies and approaches to overrule the fight or flight reaction and make more positive choices and decisions. This is where we will go now, to think about the positive strategies we can put in place to build a happy and fulfilling life in our new environment.

 Reflection time 8.1

What do you notice about how you are currently thinking, feeling and behaving?

Why acknowledging our needs matters

We all possess a range of needs that we are motivated to achieve. Maslow introduced the 'hierarchy of needs', suggesting that humans have an order in which these needs must be met.[68] At the bottom of the hierarchy are the basic existence needs: food, drink, comfort, warmth, safety and security. Then, at the next level, we need to relate, to create meaningful connections and to be recognized and validated from external sources. The third level represents our need for personal development and self-actualization.

Increasingly psychologists are finding evidence to suggest that our needs can operate on many levels simultaneously rather than in the hierarchical format that Maslow suggested. For example, satisfaction of our social needs does not need to follow that of our basic existence needs.[69] Consider the strategies in this chapter within the context of these needs:

- existence needs (hunger, thirst, warmth, comfort, safety, security);
- relatedness needs (social and intimate relationships, social connectedness, external validation); and
- growth needs (personal growth and development, realizing personal potential, work or activities that give a sense of purpose and meaning).[70]

Which needs matter to you and how can you best meet them?

To support you as you adjust to your new life abroad, we offer two broad frameworks. The first involves thinking about the needs that you're motivated to achieve and building strategies to do just that. The second involves thinking about how you can build your resilience by returning to the Four Ps highlighted in the introduction.

Recognizing what you need and some suggested strategies

Existence needs

How you satisfy these needs will depend on where you are living in the world.

Food and drink: For many expats, finding the foods they want can be an initial challenge; recognizing them in supermarkets in different packages and languages can be tough. In some countries, it can be difficult to get hold of the food you like, or you may have to cope with food shortages and limited supplies. Over time you will adjust to using what is available. For some this is part of the fun; for others, part of the pain.

Comfort and relaxation: Spend time making your house a home. Then it will be your sanctuary, a place where you can escape and recharge your batteries following days out on the front line of cultural assimilation and adjustment.

It is important to take time out to relax and recharge. For assignees, it can be tempting to stay connected 24/7. Build time into your schedule when phones and laptops are switched off. Create blocks of time away from the work environment. Engage in activities that enable you to disconnect completely from your work role. As the partner, take time out to do things that you enjoy. You need to de-stress as well.

If you have moved with children, give them autonomy over their rooms. Involving them in the process and allowing them to make choices will help them to feel they have some control in the whole relocation experience.

Safety and security: Wherever you are in the world, it pays to learn about this aspect of your life and take care. If you are living in a potentially challenging country, politically or economically, discuss what level of risk or kind of event would make you wish to leave. Ensure that you have sufficient funds for departure, and know how to arrange your departure. Organizations with sizeable expat populations do regular risk assessments and have evacuation procedures in place. If you don't know your organization's policy, ask.

Relatedness needs

We've already underscored the importance and value of building support networks in your new local community. It can take time to find people that you connect with, but it is important to persevere for all the reasons mentioned earlier. For a list of clubs and groups around the world go to the Thriving Abroad book membership area.

Language: Not all expats learn the local language fluently. However, many do learn enough to be able to manage daily life and find it pays dividends in helping them to understand the local culture and behaviour. It's also a good way to make friends and to get to know the local community. It does take time and commitment, and it's important to set the right expectations. One hour of grammar a week will not make you a fluent speaker. Be prepared to get out and speak to people, make mistakes and learn experientially as well as through formal lessons and textbooks. You will generally find that the local population appreciate the effort you make.

Children and social connections: It can take time for children to settle in to new social groups as well. As parents, we want life to be perfect for them as soon as we arrive. But it takes time, and you may find your children cycle through highs and lows as they form different friendships and attach themselves to different groups. Try not to have too many expectations, and be there to support and talk as and when needed. It may help for them to hear about your experiences as well, so they know it's not 'just them'.

It is also important to remember that a child's or teen's perspective on a move will not be the same as yours. Their world view is very different. Things that are obvious to us may not be obvious to them. For example, young children are not able to understand the context of the process involved in a move. Parents will report that their young children, after a while, ask, 'When are we going home?' They relate the experience to one that they already know, such as a holiday – which has an end and return date.

Kate Berger, adolescent psychologist, consultant and the founder of Expat Kids Club, recommends remembering that children have not chosen to make a move. They may feel removed from the decision-making process, frustrated or angry. They may also see parents going through difficulties, stressed by the experience, and this can make them feel insecure and unsettled. For more information about effective parenting in transition, listen to the interview with Kate Berger on the Thriving Abroad podcast.

Relationship with your partner: Make time to spend together. It can be easy to lose the connection if your experiences are different. If you're both working, you will have different work environments and challenges. If one partner is not working formally, then the daily stresses and strains will appear very different. Seek to understand the experience from each other's perspectives. Respect that it's not a question of who is having the most stressful time but a question of how you can acknowledge the experience of the other and provide ongoing support.

Recognize when you or a loved one needs professional help. Often we think it is a sign of weakness to ask for help. It is not. If things are getting too much and you are not sleeping, eating, you are short tempered, feel consistently down or depressed, overwhelmed and unable to focus, or are finding yourself reaching for that comforting glass of wine a little too often then it may be time to seek professional help. You will not be the first or last expat to do so, we promise. There are professional counsellors who understand the relocation process, the stresses involved and who will be able to support you through the transition.

Growth needs

We talk more about the developmental and growth-related nature of the relocation experience in the following two chapters. For the partner who is not officially working this can be a pertinent issue. For both employee and partner it is worth thinking about how you want this experience to develop new skills, knowledge and talents. Where do you want to develop professionally during your time abroad? And how will you integrate new skills in terms of language and global leadership into your future career and life trajectory?

 Reflection time 8.2

What do you notice about your personal needs in relation to your existence, relatedness and growth needs? How can you better meet those needs?

Support provided by your organization

In Chapter Four we talked about the scope of global mobility (GM) policies in organizations. Hopefully you are fully aware of the core benefits that you and your partner and family are receiving from your organization.

Some companies, though by no means all, will be prepared to provide additional settling-in support once you've arrived in your host country, such as:

- cultural training and coaching;
- executive coaching (for the assignee);
- life and career coaching (for the expat partner);
- financial support (for the expat partner's professional training or re-training);
- language training (for the assignee, partner and family);
- mentorship (identifying local host country nationals or expats to help you settle into your new environment).

The scope and extent of this support will vary and may not be explicitly mentioned, but this doesn't mean it will not be made available. If you have additional support needs, it is always worth checking with your organization and finding out what is possible. Their investment in your relocation has been substantial; for them, it pays to support your adjustment.

It is worth noting there is a current trend among organizations to offer lump-sum relocation benefits, where assignees and their families are given a relocation budget and a menu of options for spending it. Thus, organizations are transferring the responsibility of choosing appropriate support in some areas to the assignee. If you receive this type of package, you will have more flexibility to acquire the support you need.

Support that you create for yourself

In this section, we utilize the value of the Four Ps outlined in the introduction and demonstrate how they can create the foundation of your adjustment to and resilience towards your new life abroad:

- **P**ositivity
- **P**roactive
- **P**urpose
- **P**ersonal development

In Chapter Two, we mentioned that resilience was a benefit of international relocation. Resilience is the process of adapting well in the face of adversity. It is a behaviour that can be learned and developed. Here, we outline four strategies that can be used to develop your resilience.

The value of positivity and a proactive approach

First, let's discuss how you can harness the power of positivity and a proactive approach to support your transition through the adjustment process. The matrix below shows *Proactive* on the horizontal axis, low to high, and *Positivity* on the vertical axis, low to high.

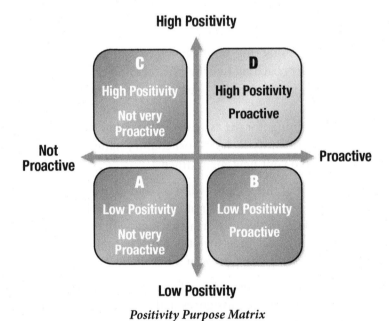

Positivity Purpose Matrix

According to the *Oxford English Dictionary*, being proactive means 'creating or controlling a situation rather than just responding to it after it has happened'.

And according to Barbara Fredrickson, positivity is 'an encompassing word that is used to refer to a wide range of positive emotions such as love, joy, gratitude, interest and hope'.[71]

But this approach is not about always being positive. We are not talking about the happy *fake it till you make* it kind of approach. Rather, it is the ability to embrace what Fredrickson refers to as the big ten emotions: love, joy, gratitude, serenity, interest, hope, pride, amusement, inspiration and awe. These can lead to feelings of positivity and happiness. Developing positivity and emotions such as gratitude can be a good antidote to stress.[72]

This matrix shows how positivity and proactivity can combine to create powerful and effective behaviour.

The person in quadrant A is not very proactive and has little positivity. Knocks hit them hard. A bad experience may create negative thoughts and emotions, which they then ruminate on and allow to multiply. As this person is not particularly proactive, they are less likely to actively seek a way of improving their emotions, thoughts or behaviours. You can see how a vicious cycle of negativity could result.

The person in quadrant B is proactive but low in positivity. They may take action but negatively interpret the resulting experiences. A focus on what has gone wrong, and a lack of hope and belief in what is possible, can have the impact of closing down their minds and emotions.

The person in quadrant C is high in positivity, choosing hope over fear, but not particularly proactive in getting out and building a new life in their new environment. The sad result can be loneliness and isolation, and missing out on the great opportunities and experiences that are available if they would just look for them.

The person in quadrant D is proactive and has higher levels of positivity. They are more likely to approach the adjustment process openly, with hope and enthusiasm. As Fredrickson says, to be open is to 'let go of rigid expectations and expand our awareness from all our senses'.[73]

This seems to us a fantastic approach to adopt when adjusting to your new context and environment.

Reflection time 8.3

Where would you place yourself on the matrix of positivity and proactivity?

What can you do to be more proactive and live with more positivity?

Developing your personal capability

One of the most amazing benefits of international relocation is the developmental opportunity, from both a personal and professional perspective.

In Chapter Five, we outlined the Five Pillars for making your relocation decision. Personal resources is one of them. It may be interesting to look back on what you wrote then and compare that list to the one you would write today.

As Paul discovered when he talked to Jean, through international relocation you acquire powerful new knowledge and skills that will help you to manage your adjustment from a cognitive, emotional and behavioural perspective.

In the interest of simplicity, we believe that there are two main areas of personal development that will contribute hugely to your capability: developing your intercultural intelligence and your understanding of (and ability to use) your personal strengths.

Hopefully you are well under way in developing your cultural intelligence, and your company is supporting you with this. If not, you might consider taking a cultural intelligence assessment.

Irrespective of our cultural origins or awareness, we all possess personal strengths: things that we do well and that energize us.[74] Because strengths are energizing, they are motivating. We tend to enjoy the work we do that involves our strengths, and we do it well.

Utilizing our strengths should make the adjustment process a confidence-building and enjoyable experience. Research has shown that when utilizing our strengths we are happier; more confident; have higher levels of self-esteem, energy and vitality; experience less stress; are more resilient; are more engaged and perform better at work; are more likely to achieve our goals; and are more effective at developing ourselves and growing as an individual.

These are all factors that will support the adjustment process. You can find support for these two areas in the Thriving Abroad book membership area and in the resources section of this book.

 Reflection time 8.4

How are you developing your cultural intelligence?

What are your personal strengths and how are you using them as you adjust to your new life abroad?

Purpose

Throughout the book we have talked about how valuable it is to understand your 'reason why', the motivation behind your decision to relocate abroad. Now, as you work through the highs and lows of the adjustment process, it's time to bring your reason why to the fore and clarify your personal and professional goals for embarking on this international journey. This sense of purpose will motivate you through the tough moments.

Sense of purpose is also about making a commitment to act purposefully in all you do. Some people talk about the need to find their grand purpose in life. We are not so convinced about that, but what we do know is that people who are purposeful tend to achieve more and are happier. So, living and acting with purpose is important, but as Paul Dolan, author of Happiness by Design, says, it is not enough in isolation. He suggests that 'to be truly happy, then you need to feel both pleasure and purpose'. He calls this the pleasure-purpose principle.[75]

Act with purpose and also think about what activities will generate a sense of enjoyment and pleasure for you and your family. Build these activities into your lives.

 Reflection time 8.5

How can you build more purpose and pleasure into your adjustment process?

Summary

- ❑ The time after arrival and before being settled is 'a psychological no-man's land.' (William Bridges)

- ❑ The adjustment process is very important; people need to adjust in order to engage with and perform well in their new life abroad.

- ❑ Adjustment is required in all areas of your life, professional, personal and family, and in the roles that you play in each.

- ❑ You will adjust in three ways:
    - ◆ in the way you think (cognitive adjustment);
    - ◆ in the way you feel (emotional adjustment); and
    - ◆ in the way you behave (behavioural adjustment).

- ❑ Understanding the needs that you wish to fulfil will help you to identify the appropriate strategies to put in place.

❑ Support for adjustment may come from your organization or from a strategy you have created.

❑ The Four Ps (positivity, proactive, purpose and personal development), when combined, provide a good strategy for adjustment and developing resilience.

CHAPTER NINE

Thriving abroad for assignees

'We are our choices.'
Jean-Paul Sartre

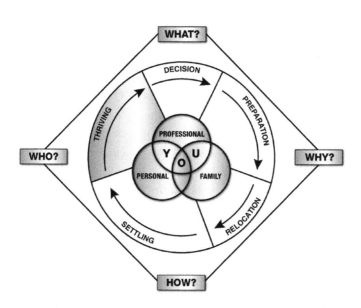

Jenny and Paul

As the plane soared into the air Jenny felt herself relax. They were finally on their way. It hadn't been an easy few months. Uncertainty about what and where next – after the China assignment – had been tough for them all to live with, and a huge pressure for her. She was conscious that it was her career that was leading the way, paying the bills and maintaining their lifestyle. Fortunately, the assignment offered seemed positive, and Jenny hoped that it would work out well for all of them. Time for some reflection. Jenny opened her notebook, having just taken up journaling as a way of releasing stress and organizing her thoughts. She wanted to write about what she had learned through the 'Chinese experience', as they all now called it.

'Have a plan,' she wrote, though, clearly, that was something she didn't have. Her plan had stopped when they got to China. It had seemed such a monumental move and change that it had been difficult to imagine life past China. She quickly became engrossed in her new role and there seemed to be no space to think past it. Time flew and suddenly they were nearing the end of the assignment with no place to go next. It was a real scramble to get in touch with human resources (HR) and start the conversations, especially as she wanted to tie in a move with the school year. Quickly she realized she had gone 'off radar'. Forgotten. To give them their credit, HR did pick things up quickly, but it wasn't ideal. This time, she was determined to keep connections with head office. In fact, she should plan regular trips back and arrange review meetings with relevant people. There was a need for both planning and flexibility, she realized. So, how did she feel about the new move? It was a sideways one rather than the promotion she had originally hoped for. But she was pleased. The project was an exciting one and the location, Singapore, worth the compromise. Paul was delighted; he already had interviews lined up and was determined to get back to work. This would take the financial pressure off Jenny for a while, and as the role was not going to be as challenging, hopefully she would have more time to spend with the children.

This chapter is written for assignees, and encourages you to focus on the professional aspect of international relocation. Take time to reflect on the role and how the experience is shaping up, to build in a regular review process, look to the future, and think about and plan for what will come next. As Jenny's story illustrates, it is easy to become engrossed in the here and now and neglect to influence the future.

GM professionals interviewed in the research stage of preparing this book all emphasized the importance of employees' taking a proactive approach in managing their long-term careers.

For Jenny, it worked out in the end. But some assignees talk about being sent back to home-based, lacklustre roles that fail to use any of their newly minted international skills; some feel they have been forgotten abroad and come to the end of their assignment with nowhere to go next. There is often an assumption that the organization will look after them, but this is not always the case. Even if the organization is looking out for you, it pays to play an active part. The truth is that 'out of sight often does mean out of mind. Bosses over-reward the people they meet every day compared with those rarely seen around the office.'[76]

Then there are the stories of assignees at odds with their partners about what they want next. The assignee assumes that another international move would be just the ticket, while the partner is counting down the days until they can go home.

This chapter helps you to build a process of review so that you can remain on top of your career management. This will mean that you avoid the possibility of drift, and of your future being determined by someone else's agenda and priorities. The ideal would be to work with your GM and/or talent management team to identify the next best steps for you and your organization, one that links to a clear purpose and delivers value to both.

The first part of this chapter looks to the process of review, the second to career development, so that you can influence positively your organization's recognition of your performance and plan positively for your next career move.

Managing the professional aspect of the assignment experience

Making time to conduct a regular career review will mean that when you need to demonstrate your value or update your résumé or career story, you will have the data immediately to hand. We recommend considering career issues frequently. This will enable you to check that you are on track and moving forward in all the areas that are important to you, identify any challenges and create strategies to deal positively with them.

 Reflection time 9.0

How is this assignment working out professionally?
- *Where are you on track?*
- *Where are you not on track?*

- *What needs to change?*
- *What professional development or learning objectives do you have?*

Tracking performance: why it's important

From a professional perspective, identifying a way to track your performance will help you to self-evaluate your progress and accomplishments. This can be a tough exercise to do retrospectively, especially if you've left it for a few years. Tracking your professional wins as they occur will save you time and heartache later.

However, it's not just your personal assessment of your performance that is useful. It's also important that your organization observes and recognizes your contribution. Gaining clarity on what you're doing and achieving will be great preparation for conversations about your role outcomes and future career direction.

Tracking performance: how it's monitored

How clear are you about how your performance will be monitored and your results recognized?

In Chapter One we talked about how organizations measure the return on investment from international assignments. Research finds that the only consistent measure by the majority of companies is cost-effectiveness. Others may make a connection between enhanced sales or profits and the assignee, but these are often based on tenuous connections between contribution, performance and outcome.[77]

If you (or your organization) want to be able to demonstrate performance, there needs to be agreement on the desired outcomes of the assignment. From your perspective, it is helpful to have clarity about what you want to achieve and what your contribution and added value is likely to be. Think back to the conversation about success factors in Chapter One. What did you identify there from a professional perspective?

There are two relevant questions to answer in relation to the way in which your performance is monitored: What will the *process* of evaluation be for you? And *what* will be evaluated?

Often, home-based annual performance reviews are used for international assignees. While there is a lot of debate generally about the value of this kind of review process, their use will depend on your organization's philosophy and practice. Whether this is a formalized process or not, you will want to be able to demonstrate in some way your contribution. The challenge with in-house reviews is that they do not usually account for the context of your international situation.

We suggest you think about what aspects of the international context and associated challenges should be understood. Also, think about how you feel your performance should be assessed in order to accurately reflect the contribution you make, and the value you add in the short, medium and long term. Bear in mind that while some aspects of your output may be tangible, some will not.

Consider both tangible and intangible aspects of your experience. Contributions that could be considered include:

- your performance in relation to role goals and objectives;
- the development of your capabilities in terms of skills and knowledge (remember global mindset and cultural skills);
- the contribution you make to the internationalization or expansion of your organization;
- the development of wider global networks and relationships;
- the knowledge and experience that you share with colleagues both abroad and back in your home country; and
- your potential in terms of future career development and the support you will provide in terms of global mindset and leadership capabilities.

Gone are the days where an international assignee's future was assured simply because they accepted an international assignment. Also, gone in large part are the paternalistic organizations that hold the assignee's hand and manage their future career development for them. Performance and results now count.

 Reflection time 9.1

How will your performance be monitored? Does this fully represent your contribution? If not, what suggestions can you make to improve the overall assessment of the value you provide?

Looking to the future

Rich and Angela

Rich was furious. He was a month away from the end of his assignment and without any discussion had just been informed that he would be returning home to his previous role. What? Angela had finally settled and was loving life in London – she wouldn't be keen on returning home after all the effort she had put into building her life here. But what choice did they have? It seemed no one back home had any concept of the work he had been doing, including HR. He had put his heart and soul into the role and built a cohesive European finance team, creating great collaboration and support. Rich knew he'd made a very positive impact, but no one in head office seemed to value this contribution. They didn't seem to get the cultural nuances and challenges of working in Europe. He had come such a long way since striding in with his US-centric plans two years ago. Now he would be going back to the US office to a US-focused role; where was the sense in that? Rich sighed. He knew that Angela was going to suggest he looked for a new role in London. That opened up another can of worms. The last time he had updated his CV was over three years ago, and to whom would he send it anyway? He had no job search contacts in the UK. He'd never had the need.

Poor Rich! His next step was defined without his consultation, or indeed, without any consideration of his performance or the skills he had acquired in terms of leading a culturally diverse team. Surprising but not uncommon. Repatriation statistics show that many companies have depressing retention figures for returning internationals for exactly this reason.

Rich, quite rightly, can be annoyed – to a point. The blame can't be laid wholly at his employer's door. Organizations are increasingly expecting employees to take part of the responsibility in securing the next steps.

This reflects the general view that the paternalistic relationship of old, where the organization was the key stakeholder and the employee a resource to be allocated as strategy and business operations demanded, is changing. Increasingly, the employer–employee relationship is one of partnership, where it is recognized that both employees and organizations have needs best met through collaboration and discussion.[78]

This approach puts the employee more in the driving seat and emphasizes their need to clarify what they want from their professional life. It is not the employer making career decisions and fitting the employee to those decisions; it is the individual who decides which opportunities to seek, which pathways to follow and what learning to pursue.[79]

The more fluid, employee-centred approach is underpinned by the reality that organizations are no longer so hierarchical. Flatter organizational structures mean that future career progression is not going to always be upwards and linear. Jenny accepted her sideways career move, recognizing the benefit of some years of consolidation after the challenging years in China. Rich was not so happy, but this was because the new role would fail to use his international experience – understandably frustrating.

It is becoming increasingly accepted for careers to take a more variable path. An employee could move within an organization over time in a horizontal, vertical or diagonal path. The focus is on the challenge, on the learning and development; it shifts away from the belief that the 'only way is up'. Someone might go from a business unit to a new geographical location, to the head office, to another division, creating a career lattice which creates many options that the traditional vertical approach cannot.[80]

Even when organizations have the best of intentions, there are no long-term guarantees of employment. It is important to be conscious of the need to build employability for internal and external purposes, to develop skills that are not location or organization specific.[81] There is one certainty: your future will involve some form of change.

As Jenny pointed out, it can be uncomfortable to live with uncertainty. What seems to impact many international assignees and their families negatively is the 'lack of knowing' what will come next. The thought of having to work through the change process all over again can also seem challenging. It takes effort and involves risk.

There are two ways to handle this uncertainty.

The first way is to put your head in the sand and ignore it. For many, as with Rich and Jenny, this is an easy strategy, as living abroad can be an all-engrossing experience. It takes time to settle and adjust, and just as you feel you are 'getting there', it's time to move on again. Without meaning to, you let two or three years pass by thinking about what happens next only in the most general of terms.

The second way to is to be prepared. It would be wrong to say that you can plan your way to certainty; international careers don't always work that way. But this doesn't mean that all personal strategy and planning should go out of the window. It is possible to make intrinsically motivated career changes (understanding your personal why) and respond constructively to uncertainty and unplanned change. This is the concept that Robert Pryor and Jim Bright, authors of *The Chaos Theory of Careers,* call being 'luck ready.'[82]

They suggest there are eight dimensions of luck readiness which form the psychological basis of being able to respond constructively to uncertainty in your life or career:

- flexibility;
- optimism;
- risk taking;

- curiosity and open mindedness;
- persistence, especially in overcoming barriers;
- self-efficacy;
- strategic thinking; and
- belief.

Some of these dimensions may look familiar to you. In Chapter Two we talked about the benefits of international mobility and listed many of the attributes and strengths that assignees, partners and families develop from their experiences abroad. There are similarities, and perhaps you're on your way to being 'luck ready' – already!

Being 'luck ready' means having a high level of clarity about who you are and what you bring to the party, and then being prepared to face the future with an open and positive mindset as you look for the opportunities.

Moulding the future you

Your future professional success may depend on your ability to repackage and reshape your skills and identity. International relocation will have taught you to consider your career in the context of your overall life experience. Now you must ask yourself, 'How can I develop my future career in a way that suits my life choices, interests, professional goals and personal values?' and 'How can I evolve in a partnership with my employer?'

Many assignees are motivated to accept an international assignment because they want to acquire and develop their individual skills and abilities and career value, collectively their 'career capital'. Career capital is composed of three types of capabilities that put the employee in a better position to make a difference in their roles now and in the future. The three types are as follows.[83]

- *'Knowing how' career capabilities:* relate to the skills, knowledge and understanding that are needed to perform well in a role.
- *'Knowing who' career capabilities:* relate to your network and professional and social relationships, both intra- and inter-company.
- *'Knowing why' career capabilities:* relate to the motivation and energy for undertaking a role; to your sense of purpose, reason why and commitment. These capabilities provide the confidence, energy and self-assurance needed to follow a particular career direction.[84]

As we have seen, organizations are becoming increasingly aware of the challenge of managing the careers of their international assignees and recognize the need to work in partnership with international assignees to ensure the most positive outcomes following an assignment. It is a complex issue, and one that depends on the organizational structure of HR/global talent management – on how effectively they can influence the recruitment and selection of international assignees in associated companies. It also depends on the changing business needs of the organization and motivation of the employee.

You must judge how best to work with your organization. Possessing clarity about what you want next will help direct future conversations. Developing this understanding is where we go to next.

Developing your strategy for career success

You may be wondering what future career positions you would like, and what is possible. In order to secure the roles you want, you need to know who you will need to influence.

Remember the four questions situated around the Framework for Thriving Abroad: what, why, how and who. We now focus our attention on how they come into play.

What

What do you want? What is important to you? We can be pulled by what is important to others and take a largely reactive response, or we can be driven by what is important to us and combine that with what is important to others.

The former of these two options is probably the easier one. The problem is that if we continue to let other people's priorities and needs pull us, we may find that over time we lose a connection to what really matters to us. We lose ourselves to the process.

It is worth spending time identifying what really matters to you. There is an image of expat success as an endlessly exciting and often privileged life – comfortable homes, maids and drivers, first-class travel, private education for children and professional 'status' as a global leader. However, alongside this image are stories of washed-up executives whose fast-track train to expat success departed long ago. They are marginalized, demoralized, wondering how can they make their 'way back'. They're either struggling to keep up abroad, or have returned to 'less than' roles back home.

Where did they lose themselves and their aspirations along the way? Did they sign up to an image of the expat life that in reality exists for only the lucky few?

As international mobility evolves in organizations, a medium- to longer-term international assignment is no longer the only way for employees to gain international exposure, or to play international leadership roles. Remember the table in Chapter Two. What aspects of international mobility are important to you?

The 'what' does really matter.

Time to reflect and ask yourself what truly motivates you to do what you do. Understanding your personal motivations and values will not only help you make decisions about your future, but will also help you show up more authentically in everything you do. This will help with building new effective relationships of trust on the road to career success.

> 'Life may be all taxis and airport departure lounges, but grounding outside of the world of multinationals, whether it be through family, friends or otherwise, is critical. Successful global executives are grounded in their own values, and bring those to work with them every day.'[85]

 Reflection time 9.2

What is most important to you? What grounds you in life? What role does international mobility play in meeting those priorities?

Now turn to the other three questions in the Framework for Thriving Abroad; why, how and who and consider your career and professional development within the overall context of continued global mobility.

Why

By understanding our why, we create energy and motivation for what we do as described by the career capital model above.[86] Your international career impacts on all aspects of your life. It is the reason for the relocation, for the transition of your life from one country to another. In thinking about the future, gain clarity about the purpose and meaning of your international journey.

In Chapter Five we asked you to think about your reason why for taking the international assignment. Motivations change over time. You will find that you value different things at different stages in your life. Understanding what is important to you will help you to identify what you want to do next and your reason for doing so.

Think beyond the motivations of career, money and adventure and go deeper to understand what inspires you to continue your international life. Think about this in the three core areas of your life: personal, professional and family.

How

How are you going to make the changes that you want or need to make? Understanding your goals and then creating a plan of action is the first step.

You will also benefit from having a clear understanding of your personal resources and how they will help you to move forward in your international life and career if this is what you choose.

Have you taken a complete inventory of your skills and knowledge? Whatever you choose to do from this point on, it is important to understand your capabilities and have the self-awareness to be able to describe them. Who are you in terms of your skills, knowledge, strengths and talents? Who do you need to be to lead effectively in your professional and personal life?

Taking time to do a personal capability audit is valuable because:

- understanding your capabilities is an essential piece in the confidence puzzle;
- it will identify what you need to develop in your pursuit of lifelong learning and enhanced professional competence; and
- it will enable you to present your capabilities more effectively through your CV and career story when required.

Who

Your network and how you develop it will have an impact on your success professionally and personally. Of course the two are interlinked and extend beyond borders. In his article on successful international executives, Simon Hayes says the following:

> 'As businesses move away from traditional command-and-control structures, and towards more dispersed modes of operation, power tends to move with the network, rather than the title. Influential executives think about the way they work with others, and the scope and scale of their internal and external networks.'[87]

In Chapter Eight we discussed how valuable social networks are in the adjustment process. Networks also have an important role to play in your evolving career and personal success. Take time to invest in relationships, to support others and build your personal and professional tribes.

 Reflection time 9.3

Identify your reason for continuing (or not continuing) your international lifestyle.

How will you work proactively to create the future you want?

Who in your professional and personal networks can help you?

Keeping it current

Earlier in the chapter we noted the value of recording your accomplishments regularly. This is where implementing that practice will pay dividends. Rich has no current résumé. He is not alone in this respect. Creating or updating your résumé is hardly top of the list when managing an international relocation and settling into a challenging new job – understandable, but perhaps a little crazy when you sit back and think of the heightened career risk involved in relocating to work abroad. It makes sense to spend some time mitigating that risk. And we are not necessarily talking about creating a résumé to help you find work outside your current organization. It is also helpful to have your résumé updated for internal career opportunities as well.

Here are a few tips for keeping yourself current and ready to roll, should the need arise.

- Keep your résumé up to date. Review your accomplishments regularly and add them to your résumé. Make sure that you make them specific and outcome related.
- Keep your social media profiles up to date and ensure they contain the kind of information you're happy to share professionally. In particular, keep your LinkedIn profile current (a nice photo, a summary which reflects your skill set, and bullet points under each role heading so that people get a sense of who you are and what you do). Join relevant groups and play an active role in the discussions. Perhaps even take advantage of LinkedIn Pulse and write some articles on a subject of professional interest to you.
- Keep your connections up to date, at home and abroad. Use online and offline networking events and opportunities. Remember that networking is about offering your expertise or connections to help and support others. Make time to nurture all your organizational connections.

Studies have shown that assignees often neglect the home-based connections and then find they have fallen off everyone's radar. Plan to return to your home base a few times a year to attend conferences and professional meetings and to reconnect with key influencers in your organization.

- Engage in professional development. Keep learning. You can do this in many ways – online, through local courses or through more formal, structured professional programmes.
- Find a mentor in your organization who will support you in your career development and role abroad.
- Work with a career coach to appraise your progress, review accomplishments, identify your next career and developmental steps and develop a strategy of action for achieving those goals.

 Reflection time 9.4

What do I need to do to ensure I am prepared optimally for securing my next position, either in my organization or externally?

Summary

- ❑ Time will fly by. Change is inevitable. Are you change ready?

- ❑ It's important to be proactive in determining how your value will be assessed. Don't leave it to pre-determined, home-based systems that do not reflect the international context and challenges of your role.

- ❑ Luck readiness is a valuable strategy and calls on eight personal dimensions: flexibility, optimism, risk taking, curiosity and open mindedness, persistence, self-efficacy, strategic thinking and belief.

- ❑ The organizational–employee relationship is changing from one of paternalism to partnership or dual dependency.

- ❑ Many organizations take a more employee-centred approach, allowing careers to take a number of variable paths.

- ❑ The career capital model[88] considers the career assets that employees bring to successive employment settings. It is a helpful model in defining both the benefits and value of international assignment as a longer-term career strategy.

CHAPTER TEN

Thriving abroad for the expat partner

'The obstacle in the path becomes the path. Never forget, within every
obstacle is an opportunity to improve our condition.'
Zen parable

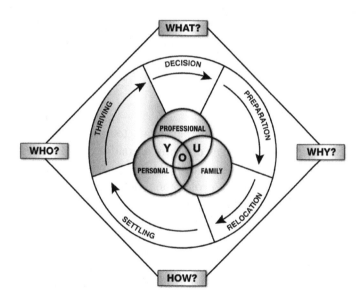

Rich and Angela

It was during one of her Sunday morning chats with her mum that Angela realized she had to get her act together. Her poor unsuspecting mum made a comment about her life of leisure. She was surprised that Angela had not been more proactive in looking for work in London. Since her divorce, her mum had continually emphasized the importance of career and financial independence. On reflection, this was probably one reason why Angela was feeling so uncomfortable relying on Rich for everything. She finally admitted, albeit angrily, that her mum was right. She needed to find a job and continue to develop her career. She had thought a career break would be fun, no need to get up, no stress, and yet its absence created a different kind of stress. Angela had envisaged a full life of travel and social events, but the reality was quite different. The new role for Rich was a big step up and extremely challenging. If he wasn't away travelling he was in the office working, and Angela was home alone much of the time. When she did get to socialize with Rich's colleagues, Angela was referred to as 'Rich's wife'. It was as though she had become 'a nobody'. People were nice enough, but no one saw her for who she was. She had to get going and sort out her career; she realized it was totally up to her – she had to make the first moves, the connections. The question was, where to start?

As the accompanying partner you may relate to some of these sentiments. When asked about the challenges of living abroad, expat partners frequently cite the issue of feeling there is something lacking in their lives. For some there is clarity that what is lacking is a professional outlet. For others, the clarity has not yet formed. This sense of something missing, if left over time, can lead to a sense of regret and a feeling of lost time.

It would be wrong to say all expat partners feel this way. In research we conducted in 2012, we found that 22% of the respondents, all of them expat partners, were happy with their non-working lives, pleased that they could take time to support their partners and families while living abroad. For them, at the point the survey was conducted, career was not an issue.[89]

However, 78% of our sample told us that career was important and they wanted to work in some way while abroad and yet, only 16% were in full-time employment and a further 18% working part time. This demonstrates that the dual career issue, one that organizations highlight at the recruitment stage for international assignees, is a pervasive one. It continues to impact on assignment experience and potentially assignment success.

In addition, Generation Y, the millennials (born between 1980 and 2000), are taking over the assignment baton. They have grown up with a belief that career is important irrespective of gender. One partner sacrificing their career for the benefit of the other is not as readily accepted as it was 30 years ago. Also, for many couples, it's a financial necessity that both partners work, something we predict will become more of an issue as GM budgets and therefore benefit levels continue to be cut.

We believe that the dynamics of the dual career question go beyond the issue of 'job search and provision' for the expat partner, as this contribution from one of our survey respondents demonstrates:

> 'People in general do not understand the difference between job opportunities and a career. They just think that you should be willing to take whatever is available e.g. teaching. While my partner is making career progression, my career has just come to a standstill.'[90]

This chapter provides you with the structure and space to think about what you want from your international experience. There are no right or wrong answers to any of the questions we ask – only the answers that ring true to you. Please read this chapter with an open mind. Do not assume we are judging you, or prescribing how we think you should live your life. We are not. We present information and opinions, using the comments and shared experience of the participants to our Career Choice and the Accompanying Partner Survey, and ask questions to help you determine how you want to maximize the opportunities your international experience offers.

Take this time to pause and consider what you want for yourself, and whether a career or professional role is part of that vision. We share examples and advice from expat partners and suggest strategies to support you in creating a life that is enjoyable and fulfilling for you.

How is your life abroad serving you now?

Now that you have lived in your current location for a while, it is helpful to think about how your new life is serving you. We know, as past expat partners ourselves, the support role can be extensive during the relocation and settling-in phases. Now it's time to think about *you* and identify what you want this experience to mean from a personal and professional perspective.

Reflection time 10.0

What is working for you right now and what is not?

Challenges for expat partners

In this section, we consider the challenges partners face as they develop their new lives abroad.

The personal identity question: Who am I?

One of the biggest challenges experienced by Angela, and one of the most often cited by partners generally, is the impact that relocation has on an individual's sense of who they are, their personal identity. Our concept of self is developed through childhood and evolves as we move through the different stages of life, influenced by the roles that we play, our culture, our personal beliefs and our values.

When we move abroad, social connections change. And for many partners, careers and professional interests are left behind. As Angela described, we become, X's mum or dad, Y's partner. While the essence of who we are may not change, the part of our identity that is linked to our professional roles and community involvement is affected.

While we recognize the valuable role that we play in supporting our partners and families, we can be left with a niggling sense of restlessness. This restlessness may relate to a lack of direction and meaning in some part of our lives, and this can impact on our sense of fulfilment.

No time to pursue a conventional career

If you have children and a partner who works long hours or travels extensively for work, the responsibilities of home life can be all-consuming. For some partners, this is enough; for others, it is not.

> 'The uncertainty of perhaps picking up and moving, combined with the unpredictability of my partner's work schedule, and the need to be the primary caregiving parent makes it difficult to consider how to manage the full-time work/home-life balance. The accompanying spouse has already been given a non-paying job by default. It is just an issue of how fulfilling it is and if they'd like to keep it.'

Confidence takes a knock

Abroad, we can find the simplest tasks challenging, and this can make us question our abilities. Finding ourselves outside of the work environment, we no longer receive the explicit and implicit confirmation of our abilities that comes from a job well done. Although we are acquiring new knowledge and skills through the relocation and adjustment process, it is easy to fail to recognize day-to-day accomplishments, and this can impact negatively on our sense of confidence.

'There are many skills involved in moving successfully from country to country but they are not "officially" recognised and so it is easy to lose confidence in yourself as a potential employee.'

Difficulty finding networks

It can take time to find our niche in social and professional circles. We may have many acquaintances but feel we lack the connection that comes from those deeper and longer-term enduring relationships. We may miss our old community connections and feel distanced from them. It can take courage to step out and connect through professional groups in our host countries. Sometimes this is one step too far as we work hard to adjust on a family and personal level as well. It is easier to take the safest routes and do the comfortable things. For some that means staying home, mixing with a small number of expats. This fear can mean opportunities are missed.

Is it just me?

When we come up against these challenges and feel the self-doubt and lack of confidence, we may look at others around us and believe that we are the only ones feeling this way. No one else seems to be speaking about these issues. Everyone else seems to be happy and secure in their expat lives. We don't feel we should complain and yet…

The grass seems greener

Though we love our partners, we feel a little bit jealous – perhaps even resentful. Our lives have expanded in terms of the international experience but contracted from a professional perspective. We feel we have little control over our personal destiny. Uncertainty about the future, where and what next, also adds to the mix.

Our partners may be working hard, stressed out by their new professional roles with little time or compassion for our concerns. Their perceived lack of interest or unwillingness to talk means that issues that should be discussed are left unsaid, leaving resentment, misunderstanding and ill-feeling to ferment. For some, relationships suffer, leading to separation and divorce and all the associated challenges that can bring.

Career indecision

When we're feeling uncertain about the future, we may think there's no point in bothering to build a career.

> 'Uncertainty as to how long we would stay in each posting as we have been moving frequently, and a job contract that is only year to year – it has made me feel less inclined to find employment.'

Also, the very nature of expat life, the all-engrossing nature of settling in and supporting the relocation process, means that time simply flies by.

Adjusting to life without work, in spite of ourselves

To be honest, life can be very pleasant. It can be tempting to let things roll. See how things evolve. This is fine, if this is truly what makes you happy. But it is worth checking in with yourself and confirming that you're not falling into the trap of inaction and unintentional drift. You want to avoid waking up ten years down the line with regret for the career that never was.

No idea where or how to start looking for work

Like Angela, in a new country and culture, possibly a new language, where do we start in our job search process?

Finding work that is not what we want

If we're working on local terms, salaries may be low and at a level of seniority way below the level we were working at back home.

The reality of finding work abroad

In our Career Choice and the Accompanying Partner survey, we asked people about the obstacles to finding and securing employment abroad. Of course, the challenges vary depending on location and ability to speak the local language, but the following are challenges that you may recognize:

- work-visa restrictions (it may be difficult or impossible for you to secure work abroad);
- non-recognition of professional qualifications;
- language fluency required for roles (sometimes in more than one language);
- cultural challenges;
- negative perspectives on the expat status and probable short-term nature of job tenure;
- the need for flexibility in terms of working hours to meet child care needs;
- low local salaries making work seem unattractive; and
- lack of local knowledge on how to find work.

Reflection time 10.1

What challenges relating to your professional life are you currently facing or foresee in the future?

Turning challenges into opportunities

It is easy to become stuck as we observe these very real challenges when it comes to creating a fulfilling life. However, we can work to turn challenges into opportunities. Opportunities may not always come in the shape or form that you are expecting – being active and open to possibilities can pay dividends.

> 'Sometimes opportunities arise from where you least expect it. The most important thing is to never give up and have a lot of support from the one you love.'

We can choose how we perceive things. For example, one person may see the task of creating new social connections and friendships as a challenge, perhaps seeing the language and cultural differences as obstacles to creating meaningful connections. Another person may see it as an exciting opportunity to learn about different people and cultures. Neither is right or wrong, but the second perspective is more helpful in building those important networks.

Changing our perspective can also be helpful when we are feeling stuck or challenged by our situation.

In Chapter Eight we introduced you to the proactive/positivity matrix. Keeping that in mind, think about how you could change your perspective on the challenges you listed in the previous exercise. Here are some words of encouragement from our survey respondents.

1. Relocation leads to career disruption (challenge) for partners but also gives them an opportunity for a career break. It gives them time to step away from the pressures of career and focus on their children or personal interests while the other partner works: '[I] enjoy being able to be a stay-at-home Mum with less financial concerns than at home.'

2. The career pause gives time for a career rethink. The very act of stepping away from careers can be a catalyst for exciting reinvention and new opportunities in the foreign environment.

> '[International relocation gives you] the chance for complete reinvention of yourself and your life. It forces you to develop skills that you didn't know you had, helps you grow in creativity and resilience, allows you to identify what you really want in life, and opens up a whole new world of opportunities. It also kicks the s**t out of you repeatedly, but boy, do you get stronger.'
>
> 'While I am pleased with my career transition, I fully realize that having the financial safety net of not HAVING to earn a living has afforded me this chance at career reinvention. It has freed me to focus on developing and enhancing my skills, abilities and experience in my new field.'

3. Relocation allows time for personal development. On the one hand, relocating abroad can make us feel inadequate; we won't always get the cultural innuendos and we might not always understand the language. Yet, on the other hand, every time we step out of the house, turn on the news, interact with the locals, manage everyday tasks and read about the history and culture of our new country, we are learning and developing personally:

> '[I've valued] learning about the world. Living abroad has been such an eye-opening experience, I am forever grateful for the opportunity and for the lessons I'm learning.'

Reflection time 10.2

Looking at your list of challenges, can you flip the switch and spot the opportunities?

How do you want your international life to serve you in the future?

As discussed, the space that a career break brings is both a challenge and an opportunity. We recommend thinking consciously about this space and considering how you would like your career or professional life to develop, or not, while abroad.

This is important because if we do not consciously consider the issue, it is easy to just drift. Relocation and settling in, especially with children, can be a time-consuming process. We can easily fill our days with activities related to our support role and social life.

We are not suggesting that everyone should have a full-blown career, but we are suggesting that everyone needs to consciously make a choice about whether to pursue their professional aspirations. It is important to understand the reasons for these choices, and to recognize that aspirations will change over time as you progress through the different stages of your life. It is a question that warrants a conscious consideration at regular intervals, whether you are living at home or abroad.

To start this conscious process, think about what your career means to you.

What does career mean to you?

When we work with expat partners, they often talk about the impact of relocation on their professional life. If they, like Angela, have not been able to secure the job they want, they will talk about their frustrations and regret. There is often an underlying feeling that they are not able to meet their career expectations. At this point it is helpful to consider where their concept and definition of career is derived from.

You may think about career in the traditional sense of a nine-to-five job. We all have expectations about the positions we should hold and the salaries we should command. Take a moment to think about what you expect and where those expectations have come from. Often the expectations we hold are linked to beliefs constructed by our upbringing, education and culture. We come to hold those beliefs and expectations about what we should do as our own.

How would it be if you suspended those beliefs for a while and thought about what is important to you in relation not just to career in the sense of a job, but more broadly in the sense of your professional development and identity. What new beliefs and expectations might result?

Reflection time 10.3

What does your career mean to you?

What beliefs and expectations do you hold about your career?

Again, there are no right or wrong answers. The purpose of these questions is to encourage you to think broadly about what your career means to you. Often, we relate career to financial return, but does that always have to be the case? It is possible to make a valuable contribution and to develop professionally without being paid – think of all the fantastic work so many volunteers do worldwide. This is not to say that you need to give up your career and volunteer while overseas, although you may choose to do so. It is to suggest that if, for a while, the traditional approach to career must be suspended due to work-visa, language or cultural challenges, or due to personal choice, there are alternative ways in which you can develop professional skills and abilities which still count and will be relevant to your career of the future.

What will give you the sense of fulfilment that you seek in life?

Personal fulfilment is derived from many different areas of our lives. We may forgo a sense of fulfilment in one area to maximize fulfilment in another. Core to the concept of fulfilment is the sense of meaning and purpose that we gain from the activities in which we engage. If we lack this sense of meaning and purpose, then the activities we undertake seem pointless. Understanding which aspects of our lives are meaningful is linked to what we as individuals most value.

What is important to you? We can be pulled by what is important to others and respond reactively, or we can be driven by what is important to us and be more proactive. Admittedly, the former is probably easier. The problem is that if we continue to be pulled by other people's priorities and needs, we lose a connection to what matters to us. We lose ourselves to the process.

The 'what' in the Framework for Thriving Abroad emphasizes the need for research – research to understand international relocation in terms of challenges and opportunities, and to understand what is important to you in relation to your career and professional and personal life:

What is important to you?
What do you want to be, have and achieve?

These questions will help you to understand the personal values underlying your personal, family and professional aspirations and also your goals. This understanding will not only help you to make important professional decisions, but will also support you as you make future relocation decisions.

 Reflection time 10.4

Understanding your personal values is the starting point in thinking about what is next.

What is most important to you in each area of your life?

What do you need to create in your life to ensure that you are living in line with your values?

What do you want to be, have and achieve?

What are the possibilities?

You know what's important. The question now is, what's possible? We can't answer this question specifically for you, but we can offer a range of suggestions and share some stories.

Here are some ideas, from the conventional career approach to the less conventional.

- Find an opportunity to pursue your existing career in your new location.
- Identify a new career which you can develop in your new location.
- Review your skills and talents; look for a career that will fit, and be open to suggestions and experimentation. See what comes up and test it out.
- Seek to build a career or business that is portable and can move with you when you next relocate.
- Build a business locally.
- Embark on a new course of training and development as a basis for a new career move or to develop your knowledge and skills in your current professional area.
- Decide to see what 'shows up' by getting out and networking in your local area.
- Look for voluntary work; this is often a good choice if you are not able for visa reasons to work in your current location.
- Consider developing a portfolio career – one that encompasses several of the suggestions above.

Through the Thriving Abroad podcast, we have interviewed expat partners who created engaging professional interests in their lives abroad. Here we share what some of our interviewees have done. You will notice that not everything involves paid employment. Volunteering plays a big role in many partners' overseas experience. When carefully chosen and managed well, volunteering can be a great way of developing your skills while contributing to a community in need. It can also be a good way of explaining a career gap on your CV.

To inspire you, here are some of the wonderful things these expat partners have done (listen to the podcast at www.ThrivingAbroad.com/expat-podcast). They have:

- written books and created blogs related to their expat experience and other areas of interest;
- become business, career and life coaches (this is how Thriving Abroad was born);
- become psychotherapists and counsellors;
- volunteered in a wide range of roles and initiated new volunteer programmes to meet local needs;
- set up companies to offer marketing and website support for other businesses;
- become language teachers and coaches;
- continued their professions from pre-relocation days but on a consultancy or project basis;
- retrained as a chef and run restaurants while abroad;
- started and grew an educational advisory and consultancy business;
- created support networks for expats in Spain;
- created programmes to support expats in running the practical aspects of international relocation;
- created businesses in their expat locations that employ local craftspeople and direct profits back into the local communities;
- created a website to support and inform expat partners; and
- created new careers in organizations in their new home countries.

If you're now inspired to think about how you might develop your professional interests abroad, the following strategies will help you to get clearer on what that might look like.

Strategies for moving forward professionally

Find your sweet spot

There is a special synergy that occurs when you find the balance between what you enjoy and love to do, what you are good at and the opportunities available to you. Complete a Venn diagram as shown below to find your 'sweet spot'. Your relocation provides you with the opportunity to reinvent or re-engineer your professional interests, so take time to think about what truly inspires and energizes you.

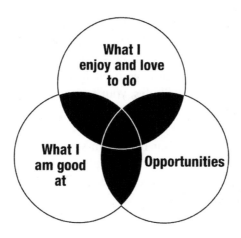

Identifying your Sweet Spot

Identify your professional direction

Earlier in the chapter we talked about the first question in the Framework for Thriving Abroad – what. Here we talk about the other three: why, how and who.

Understanding your Why

Understanding your motivation in searching for a new professional direction will mean that you move forward with a sense of purpose and commitment. It is also important to set this within the context of an international lifestyle and why it is an attractive lifestyle for you. This will link to your values, so the work you did earlier in the chapter will be helpful here. Be clear about your reason for wanting to pursue a professional interest. What makes this important to you? Then think about what you would like to do specifically and what motivates and inspires you about that choice.

How?

This question relates to the capabilities you possess in terms of your skills, knowledge and expertise and represents what you are good at. If you have not worked for a while you may begin to doubt your skills and abilities. Jacquie Kane had this advice to share during her Thriving Abroad podcast interview:

'I think the key is to approach the continuation of your career overseas with the same devotion, attention and focus that you would do if you were managing your career in your passport country. Be cognizant of professional development. I started with myself and looked at my skill-set; looked at my hard skills, looked at my soft skills, looked at the gaps. I did an assessment of my temperament; you know, there are all these online tests that people can do now – you can do your Myers-Briggs. Take the time to get to know yourself in terms of your characteristics, your values, your attributes, your personal qualities, and just list it on a piece of paper…The actual experience of relocating and moving overseas is a viable set of skills and experience and knowledge that you ought to include in your résumé in some shape or form, because it demonstrates to the prospective employer that you too can also be adaptable, fit into a new culture, be adaptable to learning new ways of doing things.'

Understand your strengths, skills and talents. We find when working with expat partners that they have often neglected to keep their CVs and career histories up to date. Now is your chance to review; build a full picture of your skills, knowledge, strengths and talents.

- What skills and knowledge did you bring with you to this international assignment?
- What skills and knowledge have you developed while you have been on assignment?
- What are your accomplishments and achievements?

Who – your networks

We need people who can support and advise us both personally and professionally. Think about the people you know both in your new and old homes. Consider how you can build appropriate networks for the goals and objectives you have. If you are considering returning to a more conventional work role, what professional networks and associations may be helpful? If you are thinking about setting up your own business, what local networks and resources are available? If you cannot find what you are looking for consider setting up something yourself. Naomi Hattaway, in her interview with the Thriving Abroad podcast talked about how volunteering doesn't have to be about joining something that already exists: 'You can fill a gap, there is no bigger confidence builder than the fact you created something that was needed.'

- Who do you know?
- Who would you like to know?
- How can you build these relationships?
- What associations or professional networks would it be helpful to join? Think about both local and international, offline and online groups.
- What could you perhaps start or initiate?

Identify your future direction

What kind of professional role would you like to pursue? There is a whole range of potential opportunities, as we have shown through the examples in this chapter. There isn't space to go through this in detail here. Investigating this in depth is something we cover in our THRIVE programme; a six month coaching programme to help expat partners create personal and professional success while living abroad.

Be proactive

Once you have decided what you would like to do, research well and then create a strategy, identify your goals and put a plan of action into place. Commit to doing one small thing each day towards achieving your goal.

 Reflection time 10.5

Using the Venn diagram, identify your sweet spot:
- *What I enjoy and love to do*
- *What I am good at*
- *What opportunities exist*
- *Identify your personal why, how and who.*

Summary

❑ This chapter will have helped initiate thoughts about the place that your professional life has, or should have, in your international experience. If you would like more support to help you define your professional path during or following international relocation, look at our THRIVE programme.

❑ While the majority of expat partners would like to work while accompanying their partners on international assignment, only a minority manage to do so.

❑ Many obstacles prevent expat partners from working abroad. In our research, we found the following to be key challenges:

 • work-visa restrictions (it may be difficult or impossible for you to secure work abroad);
 • non-recognition of professional qualifications;
 • language fluency required for roles (sometimes in more than one language);
 • cultural challenges;
 • negative perspectives on the expat status and probable short-term nature of job tenure;
 • the need for flexibility in terms of working hours to meet child care needs;
 • low local salaries (which make work seem unattractive);
 • lack of local knowledge on how to find work.

❑ Take time to think about why career is important to you. Is it the professional achievement or the monetary gain that motivates you?

❑ Opportunities do exist for expat partners, and often it's after a journey of personal discovery that they find fulfilling new career directions abroad.

❑ It is important that you identify your answers to what, why, how and who. Use these answers to help you create a professional life that you love – one that is sustainable through international transitions.

CHAPTER ELEVEN

Connecting the dots and moving forward

'Life can only be understood backwards,
but it must be lived forwards.'
Søren Kierkegaard

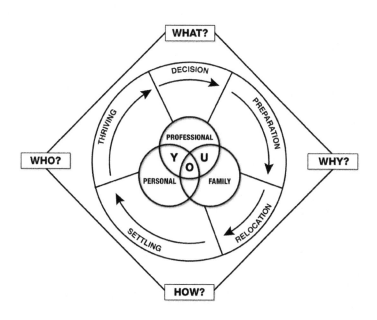

Introduction

It's been a long journey both figuratively and experientially. Our objective in writing this book was to give you a framework for thinking about the global mobility experience; to share experiences and expertise in the hope that fore-warned would be forearmed and that you would create happy and successful internationally mobile lives and careers.

The opportunity for international mobility is greater than it has ever been. International organizations are struggling to resource their need for talented individuals around the world. This need is set against an environment where GM budgets are under threat – more has to be done with less. The paternalistic organization is increasingly a feature of the past; employees partner with their employers to further organizational goals, and in so doing develop their careers. Upward mobility is no longer a guaranteed outcome of international assignment. Proactive career management is a necessity.

International relocation changes everything. In writing this book our aim was to bring the perspective of international assignees on the GM experience to the 21st century. The reality is that it's not so easy, if it ever was, but when decisions are made on the basis of sound research and an understanding of the challenges and opportunities, relocation abroad is a life-enriching experience, and not only for the assignee.

So, this is the end. It is the end of the book and perhaps the end of your first journey through the change process that relocation brings, but certainly not the end of all transition, we're sure. Perhaps you:

- are deciding whether to move to another exciting location;
- have decided to move home – repatriation can be just as challenging as expatriation (some people say more challenging); the Framework for Thriving Abroad will help you to prepare, relocate and then *thrive* in your new life back home; or
- have a decision to make about a new career move.

Here we set out the key messages of our process.

Relocation ready

It started with a dream, a desire to live abroad one day. Or maybe it started in shock and surprise as your organization invited you to consider international relocation. Whichever way it began, it led to a reaction and the beginning of a million and one thoughts, hopes and expectations.

Parts One and Two were written to help you manage the relocation decision and preparation phase – to help you manage your hopes and expectations and create an approach and strategy that would enable you to arrive and work through the initial adjustment phase in the best way possible.

We set the international career opportunity within the context of professional and personal aspirations for both the assignee and the partner.

We recognize that an internationally mobile career can take many different forms. Long-term assignments, which this book is about, are just one method of developing global management and leadership skills.

We believe the benefit of an international relocation to all stakeholders depends on the purpose, goals and objectives of the assignment. We highlighted the importance of being clear from the outset about what you're being asked to do and how capable you feel you are of performing to that level. Remember, stretch and personal development are the natural outcomes of international assignments – just don't take on too much stretch!

Importantly, the global experience should not be one that is chosen for you. The decision to embark on an assignment needs to be yours. It must be a well-researched choice, and one made jointly by the assignee and the partner.

One of the major hotspots for international assignees and their families is the issue of unmet expectations. Research and manage your expectations well and you will experience fewer disappointments and setbacks. Note that we don't say none; there will always be some. To this end, we suggested you understand the opportunities of international relocation (Chapter Two) and the hotspots and challenges (Chapter Three).

Relocating abroad is a big *life* decision, not solely a career decision. This means it is important, prior to signing on the dotted line, to understand your motivations for relocating. What aspects of your life do you hope it will improve? What are you happy to be leaving behind? What drives you to create a new, successful life and career abroad?

The assignee is not the only one affected by the relocation. This is why we wrote a book that is pertinent and accessible to both partners. Partners, as much as assignees, need to consider how the international relocation opportunity sits within the context of their personal and professional aspirations.

Change can impact on your relationship in a positive or negative way. Communication is crucial; the relocation process should encourage open communication between partners.

The relocation decision should be made on the basis of both objective and subjective thinking. The Five Pillars approach ensures that you cover all of the important areas and are able to come to an informed, joint and conscious decision. This forms the basis for assignment success.

Making it happen

Treat the preparation process as a project and aim for structure and organization.

There are two parts to the preparation process – practical and emotional. Ensure that you spend time on both.

Often the emotional aspect of preparing to relocate is ignored because the practical organization is all-consuming. Take time to say your goodbyes, and to familiarize yourself with the stages of culture shock so that you recognize the symptoms as they present themselves during the adjustment stage.

Also think about how best to prepare for the new roles that you will undertake. Remember that international relocation represents a series of simultaneous transitions and change, so be kind to yourself.

Partners, be prepared to support each other and your children through a change process that will be unpredictable and at times uncomfortable. Acknowledge each person's struggles. Compassion, empathy, good listening and understanding are the foundations of effective support and strong and trusting relationships.

Arriving to thriving abroad

Reserve some time to experience this 'new beginning' together as partners or family. Begin to build your new routines and ways of being.

Recognize the adjustment period as the change process it is – one that will be punctuated with highs and lows. Understand the impact that change has on you from a thinking, emotional and behavioural perspective.

Be open and self-aware. Be curious about the culture in which you now reside. Recognize your achievements and utilize your strengths and skills.

Be proactive in adjusting to your new professional, personal and family life. Encourage positivity in your interactions and be purposeful in all that you do. Through these behaviours you will build resilience and a positive approach to opportunity and change.

As the assignee, be conscious of and focused on your professional goals, but remember to maintain a balance between your professional, personal and family demands.

As the partner, look for ways to build a new life abroad that recognize the opportunity and honour your personal definition of a fulfilling life.

Look to the future and develop clarity about how you want GM to feature in your lives. Is this the beginning of a number of global adventures? What do you see as future opportunities and benefits for all family members?

Remember as you look forward to also acknowledge how far you have come – what you have all achieved and learned as a result of this amazing opportunity.

Our intention in writing this book was to empower you to create your own international success. We hope that the ideas and insights shared have helped you to move forward with success based on an understanding of the challenges and opportunities of this wonderful experience.

Whatever comes next for you, this book will continue to support and inspire you through change and transition to live your very best life, wherever you find yourself in the world.

Support beyond the book

We offer further support at www.ThrivingAbroad.com. Join the book membership site (www.ThrivingAbroad.com/Book), download the free workbook and browse our website to discover the support programmes we offer.

Also, go to iTunes or our blog (www.ThrivingAbroad.com/expat-podcast), and sign up for the Thriving Abroad podcast to access interviews with expats and expat experts who share fascinating stories and insights to help smooth your relocation journey. You can listen to interviews with many of the experts and expats featured in this book.

We look forward to connecting with you and supporting you through your international journey.

Glossary of global mobility terms

Allowances – compensation provided to employees to make them whole or partially whole for items which are more expensive while on assignment. These allowances are included in **home-based** and some **Local-Plus packages** for items such as housing, schooling, a cost-of-living differential and, in more challenging locations, hardship.

Destination services provider – a company or individual based in the host country which uses specialized local knowledge to help you navigate the formalities and practicalities of setting up in your new country.

Dual career – both partners in a relationship have careers they value and wish to maintain.

Home-based package – a compensation package based on compensation for the equivalent job in your **home country** and designed to keep you whole based on life in the home country. A home-based package may contain **allowances** for items such as housing, school fees, **home leave** and cost of living. Assignees on a home-based package are usually **tax equalized** to their home country. These packages are costly and complex to administer. They are becoming less common as more people become globally mobile.

Home country – the country where your contract or employment was originally based.

Home leave – a trip for you and your family to your home country for the express purpose of maintaining personal and professional ties with your home country. An annual trip to your home country is an element of many home-based relocation packages.

Host country – the country to which you are moving.

House-hunting trip (sometimes referred to as a 'look-see' visit) – a trip taken to the host country, typically once you have agreed to move there, with the express purpose of finding accommodation and schools as well as locating other services of importance to you and/or your family.

Local package – a compensation package equal to that offered to a local resident in the host country.

Local-Plus package – a basic compensation package equal to that offered to a local resident in the host country with some additional financial support for you, the international assignee. It acknowledges the greater expenses incurred by an international assignee who may not be willing to, for example, put children in the local education system.

Partner support – additional support offered to the expat partner in acknowledgement of the fact that she or he may be giving up a job or career. These support elements can include cross-cultural training and language lessons, cash allowances to support retraining, education and job search assistance and/ or career coaching to help partners find a new direction. Most packages include cross-cultural and language training for spouses but relatively few offer enhanced support for partners.

Visa – a legal permit which enables you to reside and in some cases work in your host country. It is important to know what rights are conferred by your visa, particularly if you are a dependent spouse or partner of an international assignee, as visas for dependents often do not confer the right to work.

Resources

Books

International relocation, repatriation and global careers

M. Brayer Hess & P. Linderman, *The Expert Expat: Your guide to successful relocation abroad* (Nicholas Brealey, 2007).

W. Bridges, *Managing Transitions: Making the most of change,* 3rd edn. (Da Capo Lifelong Books, 2009).

Dr C. Brubaker, *The Re-Entry Relaunch Roadmap: A creative workbook for finding happiness, success & your next global adventure after being abroad* (Thinking Travel Press, 2016).

T. Carter & R. Yates, *Finding Home Abroad: A guided journal for adapting to life overseas* (Summertime, 2014).

M. Dickman & Y. Baruch, *Global Careers* (Routledge, 2010).

L. A. Janssen, *The Emotionally Resilient Expat: Engage, adapt and thrive across culture* (Summertime, 2013).

M. Javidan & J. L.Walker, *Developing Your Global Mindset: The handbook for successful global leaders* (Beavers Pond Press, 2013).

E. Marx, *Breaking Through Culture Shock* (Nicholas Brealey, 2001).

Y. McNulty & K. Inkson, *Managing Expatriates: A return on investment approach* (Business Expert Press, 2013).

P. O'Sullivan, *Foreigner In Charge: Success strategies for leaders* (Exisle Publishing, 2014).

R. Pascoe, *A Moveable Marriage: Relocate your marriage without breaking it* (Expatriate Press Limited, 2003).

J. Parfitt & C. Reichrath-Smith, *A Career in Your Suitcase: A practical guide to creating meaningful work... anywhere* (Summertime, 2013).

M. Peterson Fenn & H. Mulligan Walker, *Inspiring Global Entrepreneurs: Discover how to successfully set up and run your dream business in a foreign country* (Live It, 2013).

A. Martins & V. Hepworth, *Expat Women: Confessions – 50 answers to your real-life questions about living abroad* (Expat Women Enterprises Pty Ltd ATF Expat, 2011).

Culture and cultural intelligence, global mindset

D. P. Caligiuri, *Cultural Agility: Building a pipeline of successful global professionals* (John Wiley & Sons, 2013).

D. Livermore, *Leading with Cultural Intelligence: The new secret to success* (AMACOM, 2009).

F. C. Solomon & M. Schell, *Managing Across Cultures: The seven keys to doing business with a global mindset* (McGraw-Hill Education, 2009).

F. Trompenaars & C. Hampden-Turner, *Riding the Waves of Culture: Understanding cultural diversity in business* (Nicholas Brealey, 1997).

E.Vannekens-Kelly, *Subtle Differences, Big Faux Pas: Test your cultural competence* (Summertime Publishing, 2012).

To support children

For parents

D. L. Ferland, *Knocked Up Abroad Again: Baby bumps, twists and turns around the globe (Volume 2)* (Lisa Ferland, 2016).

W. Ota, *Safe Passage: How mobility affects people & what international schools should do about it* (Summertime Publishing, 2014).

R. Pascoe, *Raising Global Nomads: Parenting abroad in an on-demand world* (Expatriate Press, 2006).

D. C. Pollock & R. E. Van Reken, *Third Culture Kids: Growing up among worlds*, 2nd edn. (Nicholas Brealey, 2009).

R. Rosenback, *Bringing Up a Bilingual Child: How to navigate the 7 Cs of multilingual parenting* (Filament Publishing, 2014)

For children

V. M. Afnan Ahmad *et al.*, *Slurping Soup and Other Confusions: True stories and activities to help third culture kids during transition*, 2nd edn. (Summertime, 2013).

V. Bensanceney, *B at Home: Emma moves again* (Summertime, 2014).

S. Gilor, *Navigate the Maze of Studying Abroad* (Sharon Gilor, 2013).

L. Moorefield Evans, *Relocation Workbook: Kids on the move* (CreateSpace Independent Publishing Platform, 2014).

L. Pittman & D. Smit, *Expat Teens Talk: Peers, parents and professionals offer support advice and solutions in response to expat life challenges as shared by expat teens* (Summertime, 2012).

Personal development and resources

A. Cope and A. Bradley, *The Little Book of Emotional Intelligence: How to flourish in a crazy world*, (John Murray Learning, 2016).

S. David, *Emotional Agility: Get unstuck, embrace change and thrive in work and life* (Penguin Life, 2016).

P. Dolan, *Happiness by Design: Finding pleasure and purpose in everyday life* (Penguin, 2015).

C. S. Dweck, *Mindset: How you can fulfil your potential* (Robinson, 2012).

B. Fredrickson, *Positivity: Groundbreaking research to release your inner optimist and thrive* (Oneworld Publications, 2012).

A. Linley, J. Willars & R. Biswas-Diener, *The Strengths Book: Be confident, be successful, and enjoy relationships by realising the best of you* (CAPP Press, 2010).

J. Reed and P. G. Stoltz, *Put Your Mindset to Work: The one asset you really need to win and keep the job you love* (Viking, 2013).

D. Rock, *Your Brain at Work: Strategies for overcoming distraction, regaining focus, and working smarter all day long* (HarperBusiness, 2009).

R. Pryor & J. Bright, *The Chaos Theory of Careers* (Routledge, 2011).

P. Pullan, *Virtual Leadership: Practical strategies for getting the best out of virtual work and virtual teams* (Kogan Page, 2016).

Websites

A wide range of expat-related websites provide advice and country information, which will be indispensable for your research. They may also provide a start point for networking and building social connections in your proposed destination. There are also many in-country Facebook groups created by expats for expats. They often offer a wealth of local information and are great starting points for making new connections.

General moving and relocation support

www.ThrivingAbroad.com/Blog
The Thriving Abroad blog and podcast, where you can access interviews with expat experts and expats with insights and experiences to share

www.figt.org
A forum for globally mobile individuals, families, and those working with them

www.internations.org
A great way to build connections – InterNations hosts meetups for the internationally minded in over 390 cities around the world and has over 200 destinations guides

www.expatexplorer.hsbc.com
Home of one of the largest independent expat surveys; you will also find country guides, expat tips and insights

www.expatnetwork.com
A resource for accessing the international job market and a source of destination guides and service providers

www.expatfocus.com
A source of expat information, tips and articles

www.countryreports.org
Extensive information on the country and culture in question

www.xpatulator.com
Understand the cost of living and the purchasing power of your salary in your destination country

www.expatlifeline.com
Membership site providing access to extensive courses on organizing expat life and moving with kids

www.expatica.com
Information on life and work in Europe and some destinations further afield

www.kirstyriceonline.com
www.twofatexpats.com
Moral support, information and humour for expat partners

www.facebook.com/iamatriangleinc
Active community of expats and repats.

http://globallivingmagazine.com/
A lifestyle publication & resource for expats worldwide

www.expatchild.com
Information and resources on moving overseas with children

www.expatcareers.com
Online jobs board for expats and their partners

www.idcn.info
Dual career support for expat partners. Accessible to employees and partners of member organizations only

Experts who have contributed to this book

In relation to family law: Lucy Greenwood, LLB, Partner, International Family Law Group. www.iflg.uk.com

In relation to visa acquisition: Caron Pope, Managing Partner, Fragomen Worldwide. www.fragomen.com

In relation to wills: Neil Long, Bond Dickinson. www.bonddickinson.com

In relation to elder care: Alison Hesketh, Time Finders, Senior Life Specialists. http://timefindersuk.com

In relation to language learning: Rita Rosenback, Language Coach and Author. http://multilingualparenting.com

In relation to global mobility strategy and policy: Chris Debner, Chris Debner LLC, Strategic Global Mobility Advisory www.chrisdebner.com

In relation to global mobility policy and practice: Tim Wells, Partner, Abbiss Cadres http://abbisscadres.com

In relation to international career development: Padraig O'Sullivan, Partner, O'Sullivan Field http://osullivanfield.com

In relation to relocating with children: Kate Berger, The Expat Kids Club. http://Expatkidsclub.com

References

[1] Rick Warren, *The Purpose Driven Life: What on earth am I here for?* (Zondervan, 2012).

[2] M. McQuaid, Interview with Neil Garrett, MPPW17. Available from http://www.michellemcquaid.com/podcast/mppw17-neil-garrett/ (accessed 4 March 2017).

[3] M. Shaffer *et al.*, 'Work- and family-role adjustment of different types of global professionals: Scale development and validation', *Journal of International Business Studies*, 47(2) (2015).

[4] J. Cerdin, M. Le Pargneux, 'Career and International Assignment Fit: Toward an Integrative Model of Success', *Human Resource Management*, 48(1) (2009), 5–25.

[5] Brookfield Global Relocation Services, *Breakthrough: The future of global talent mobility. 2016 Global Mobility Trends*. 21st Annual Report. Available from http://globalmobilitytrends.brookfieldgrs.com/ - /home (accessed 23 March 2017).

[6] EYGM Limited, *Tomorrow's Workforce: Data driving mobility. 2015–16 Global Mobility Effectiveness Survey*. Available from http://www.ey.com/gl/en/services/ey-global-mobility-effectiveness-survey (accessed 23 March 2017).

[7] Brookfield Global Relocation Services, *Mindful Mobility. 2015 Global Mobility Trends*. 20th Annual Report. Available from http://globalmobilitytrends.brookfieldgrs.com/ - /home (accessed 11 April 2017).

[8] J. Romero, 'The effect of expatriate training on expatriate effectiveness', *Journal of Management Research*, 2(2) (2002), 73–77.

[9] Right Management, 'Many Managers Found to Fail in Overseas Assignments' (Right Management, 2013). Available from: http://www.right.com/wps/wcm/connect/right-us-en/home/thoughtwire/categories/media-center/Many+Managers+Found+to+Fail+in+Overseas+Assignments (accessed 7 March 2017).

[10] B. Fredrickson, *Positivity: Groundbreaking research to release your inner optimist and thrive* (Oneworld Publications, 2011).

[11] V. Frankl, *Man's Search for Meaning* (Beacon Press, 2006).

[12] C. Dweck, *Mindset: How you can fulfil your potential* (Robinson, 2012).

[13] PwC, *Talent Mobility and Beyond: The future of mobility in a globally connected world* (2011) Available from https://www.pwc.com/gx/en/managing-tomorrows-people/future-of-work/pdf/pwc-talent-mobility-2020.pdf (accessed 11 April 2017).

[14] L. Wiles & E. Simpson, Thriving Abroad Relocation Decision Survey, 2015 (Unpublished, 2015).

[15] Brookfield Global Relocation Services, *Mindful Mobility. 2015 Global Mobility Trends.* 20th Annual Report. Available from http://globalmobilitytrends.brookfieldgrs.com/ - /home (accessed 23 March 2017).

[16] PwC, Moving People with Purpose. Modern Mobility Survey, 2014. Available from. http://www.pwc.co.uk/services/human-resource-services/modern-mobility-survey/download.html (accessed 11 April 2017).

[17] M. Dickmann, RES Forum Annual Report 2015, *Strategic Management and Global Talent Conundrum* (RES Forum, 2015). Available from https://theresforum.com/wp-content/uploads/2015/04/RES-Report-2015-Introduction.pdf (accessed 11 April 2017).

[18] E. Michaels, H. Handfield-Jones & B. Axelrod, *The War for Talent* (Harvard Business Press, 2001).

[19] PwC, *Talent Mobility and Beyond: The future of mobility in a globally connected world*, 2011. Available from https://www.pwc.com/gx/en/managing-tomorrows-people/future-of-work/pdf/pwc-talent-mobility-2020.pdf (accessed 11 April 2017).

[20] Brookfield Global Relocation Services, *Mindful Mobility. 2015 Global Mobility Trends.* 20th Annual Report. Available from http://globalmobilitytrends.brookfieldgrs.com/ - /home (accessed 23 March 2017).

[21] M. Dickmann, RES Forum Annual Report 2015, *Strategic Management and Global Talent Conundrum* (RES Forum, 2015). Available from https://theresforum.com/wp-content/uploads/2015/04/RES-Report-2015-Introduction.pdf (accessed 11 April 2017).

[22] P. O'Sullivan, *Foreigner In Charge: Success strategies for leaders* (Exisle Publishing, 2014).

[23] Y. McNulty and K. Inkson, *Managing Expatriates: A return on investment approach* (Business Expert Press, 2013).

[24] J. Geller & A. H. Mazor, *Global Business Driven HR Transformation: The journey continues* (Deloitte, 2011). Available from https://www2.deloitte.com/content/dam/Deloitte/ie/Documents/People/2011_global_business_hr_deloitte_ireland.pdf (accessed 11 April 2017).

[25] Brookfield Global Relocation Services, *Mindful Mobility. 2015 Global Mobility Trends.* 20th Annual Report. Available from http://globalmobilitytrends.brookfieldgrs.com/ - /home (accessed 23 March, 2017).

26 L. Wiles & E. Simpson, *Career Choice and the Accompanying Partner* (Thriving Abroad, 2012). Available on request from Thriving Abroad, http://www.thrivingabroad.com

27 P. Caligiuri, *Cultural Agility: Building a pipeline of successful global professionals* (John Wiley & Sons, 2013).

28 S. Peterson, *Multinational Leadership Migration to Growth Markets* (Heidrick & Struggles, 2012). Available from http://www.heidrick.com/~/media/Publications%20and%20Reports/HS_MultinationalLeaderMigration.pdf (accessed 28 April 2017).

29 P. Caligiuri, *Cultural Agility: Building a pipeline of successful global professionals* (John Wiley & Sons, 2013).

30 M. Javidan and J. Walker, *Global Mindset: The handbook for successful global leaders* (Beaver's Pond Press, Inc., 2013).

31 Cartus Relocation, *Talent Management and the Changing Assignee Profile*. 2013 Survey Report. Available from http://guidance.cartusrelocation.com/rs/cartus/images/2013_Talent_Management_and_the_Changing_Assignee_Profile_Survey.pdf (accessed 23 March 2017).

32 L. Wiles & E. Simpson (2012) *Career Choice and the Accompanying Partner*, 2012. Available on request from Thriving Abroad, http://www.thrivingabroad.com

33 L. Wiles & E. Simpson (2012) *Career Choice and the Accompanying Partner*, 2012. Available on request from Thriving Abroad, http://www.thrivingabroad.com

34 R. Rosenback, *Bringing Up a Bilingual Child: How to navigate the 7 Cs of multilingual parenting* (Filament Publishing, 2014).

35 R. Pryor & J. Bright, *The Chaos Theory of Careers: A new perspective on working in the twenty-first century* (Routledge, 2011).

36 T. Sharot, 'The optimism bias', *Time Magazine*, May 28, 2011. Available from http://content.time.com/time/health/article/0,8599,2074067,00.html (accessed 11 April, 2017).

37 L. Wiles (2002) *Investigating the Relationship Between Expectations and Adjustment to International Assignments*. MSc Dissertation, University of Leicester.

38 J.S. Black & G.K. Stephens, 'The other half of the picture: Antecedents of spouse cross-cultural adjustment', *Journal of International Business Studies*, 22 (1989), 461–477.

39 Brookfield Global Relocation Services, *Mindful Mobility. 2015 Global Mobility Trends*. 20th Annual Report. Available from http://globalmobilitytrends.brookfieldgrs.com/ - /home (accessed 23rd March, 2017).

40 M.A. Shaffer. D.A. Harrison, 'Forgotten partners of international assignments: development and test of a model of spouse adjustment', *Journal of Applied Psychology*, 86(2) (2001), 238–254.

[41] Y. McNulty, 'Till stress do us part: The causes and consequences of expatriate divorce', *Journal of Global Mobility*, 3 (2) (2014), 106–136.

[42] Brookfield Global Relocation Services, *Mindful Mobility. 2015 Global Mobility Trends.* 20th Annual Report. Available from http://globalmobilitytrends.brookfieldgrs.com/ - /home (accessed 23rd March, 2017).

[43] Y. McNulty, 'Till Stress do us part: The causes and consequences of expatriate divorce', *Journal of Global Mobility*, 3 (2) (2014), 106–136.

[44] L. Greenwood, International Family Law Group, Interview and correspondence (2017).

[45] A. Martins & V. Hepworth, *Expat Women: Confessions. 50 answers to your real life questions about living abroad* (Expat Women Enterprises Pty Ltd, 2013).

[46] L. Perelstein, School Choice International

[47] Kristin Louise Duncombe, *Trailing – A Memoir* and *Five Flights Up* (CreateSpace Independent Publishing Platform, 2012).

[48] A. Hesketh, TimeFinders UK, Interview and correspondence (2017).

[49] G. Glassock and A. Fee, 'The decision-making processes of self-initiated expatriates: A consumer behaviour approach', *Journal of Global Mobility*, 3(1) (2015), 4–24.

[50] L. Wiles & E. Simpson, Thriving Abroad Relocation Decision Survey, 2015 (Unpublished).

[51] G. Glassock and A. Fee, 'The decision-making processes of self-initiated expatriates: A consumer behaviour approach', *Journal of Global Mobility*, 3(1) (2015), 4–24.

[52] L. Wiles & E. Simpson (2012) *Career Choice and the Accompanying Partner*, 2012. Available on request from Thriving Abroad, http://www.thrivingabroad.com

[53] L. Wiles & E. Simpson (2012) *Career Choice and the Accompanying Partner*, 2012. Available on request from Thriving Abroad, http://www.thrivingabroad.com

[54] C. Pope, Fragomen Worldwide, Interview and correspondence (2015, 2017).

[55] L. Greenwood, International Family Law Group, Interview and correspondence (2017).

[56] N. Long, Bond Dickinson, Interview and correspondence (2015, 2017).

[57] L. Greenwood, International Family Law Group, Interview and correspondence (2017).

[58] P. O'Sullivan, *Foreigner In Charge: Success strategies for leaders* (Exisle Publishing, 2014).

[59] R. E. Van Reken, D. C. Pollock & M. V. Pollock, *Third Culture Kids: Growing up among worlds*, 3rd edn (Nicholas Brealey, 2009).

[60] A. Hesketh, TimeFinders UK, Interview and correspondence (2017).

[61] R. E. Van Reken, D. C. Pollock & M. V. Pollock, *Third Culture Kids: Growing up among worlds*, 3rd edn (Nicholas Brealey, 2009).

[62] D. Ota, *Safe Passage: How mobility affects people & what international schools should do about it* (Summertime Publishing, 2014).

[63] H. Spencer-Oatey, *Culturally Speaking: Culture, communication and politeness theory*, 2nd edn (Continuum International Publishing Group, 2008).

[64] K. Oberg, 'Culture Shock'. Talk presented to the Women's Club of Rio de Janeiro, Brazil, 3 August, 1954. Available from http://citeseerx.ist.psu.edu/viewdoc/download?doi=10.1.1.461.5459&rep=rep1&type=pdf (accessed 11 April 2017).

[65] W. Bridges, *Managing Transitions: Making the most of change*, 3rd edn (Da Capo Lifelong Books, 2009).

[66] A. Haslberger, C. Brewster & T. Hippler, 'The dimensions of expatriate adjustment,' *Human Resource Management*, 53(2) (2013), 333–351.

[67] A. Haslberger, C. Brewster & T. Hippler, 'The dimensions of expatriate adjustment,' *Human Resource Management*, 53(2) (2013), 333–351.

[68] S. McLeod, 'Maslow's hierarchy of needs' (Simply Psychology, 2007). Available from http://www.simplypsychology.org/maslow.html (accessed 16 March 2017).

[69] D. Rock, *Your Brain at Work: Strategies for overcoming distraction, regaining focus, and working smarter all day long* (HarperBusiness, 2009).

[70] Alderfer's ERG Theory. Understanding the priorities in people's needs, https://www.mindtools.com/pages/article/newTMM_78.htm (accessed 11 April 2017).

[71] B. Fredrickson, *Positivity: Groundbreaking research to release your inner optimist and thrive* (Oneworld Publications, 2011).

[72] B. Fredrickson, *Positivity: Groundbreaking research to release your inner optimist and thrive* (Oneworld Publications, 2011).

[73] B. Fredrickson, *Positivity: Groundbreaking research to release your inner optimist and thrive* (Oneworld Publications, 2011).

[74] A. Linley, J. Willars & R. Biswas-Diener, *The Strengths Book: Be confident, be successful, and enjoy relationships by realising the best of you* (CAPP Press, 2010).

[75] P. Dolan, *Happiness by Design: Change what you do, not how you think* (Avery, 2014).

[76] 'Not-so-happy returns', *The Economist* (2015). Available from http://www.economist.com/news/business/21677634-big-businesses-fail-make-most-employees-foreign-experience-not-so-happy-returns (accessed 20 March, 2017).

[77] Y. McNulty & K. Inkson, *Managing Expatriates: A return on investment approach* (Business Expert Press, 2013).

[78] D. McGuire, *Human Resource Development*, 2nd edn (Sage Publications Ltd, 2014).

[79] K. Inkson & M. Arthur, 'How to be a successful career capitalist', *Organizational Dynamics*, 30(1) (2001), 48–61.

[80] B. Harrington & D. T. Hall, *Career Management & Work–Life Integration: Using self-assessment to navigate contemporary careers* (SAGE Publications Inc., 2007).

[81] Y. McNulty & K. Inkson, *Managing Expatriates: A return on investment approach* (Business Expert Press, 2013).

[82] R. Pryor & J. Bright, *The Chaos Theory of Careers: A new perspective on working in the twenty-first century* (Routledge, 2011).

[83] K. Inkson and M. Arthur, 'How to be a successful career capitalist', *Organizational Dynamics*, 30(1) (2001), 48–61.

[84] M. Dickman & H. Harris, 'Developing career capital for global careers: The role of international assignments', *Journal of World Business*, 40(4) (2005), 399–408.

[85] S. Hayes, 'Five tips for taking on a global role'. (LinkedIn Pulse, October, 2016). Available from https://www.linkedin.com/pulse/five-tips-taking-global-role-simon-hayes (accessed 11 April 2017).

[86] K. Inkson and M. Arthur, 'How to be a successful career capitalist', *Organizational Dynamics*, 30(1) (2001), 48–61.

[87] S. Hayes, 'Five tips for taking on a global role'. (LinkedIn Pulse, October, 2016). Available from https://www.linkedin.com/pulse/five-tips-taking-global-role-simon-hayes (accessed 11 April 2017).

[88] K. Inkson & M. Arthur, 'How to be a successful career capitalist', *Organizational Dynamics*, 30(1) (2001), 48–61.

[89] L. Wiles & E. Simpson (2012) *Career Choice and the Accompanying Partner*, 2012. Available on request from Thriving Abroad, http://www.thrivingabroad.com

[90] L. Wiles & E. Simpson (2012) *Career Choice and the Accompanying Partner*, 2012. Available on request from Thriving Abroad, http://www.thrivingabroad.com

Index

About the Authors

In 2015, Louise and Evelyn sat down to write a book. They wanted to share their perspective on global mobility, which originated from their insights as expats and mentors/coaches of expats. Time and time again, they realized during their conversations with expats that there were two viewpoints of global mobility that often did not interact as effectively as they could. One was the perspective of the global mobility teams that do great work in getting people to their new locations compliantly and efficiently; the second was the perspective and lived experience of the international assignees and their families.

The adjustment challenges international assignees and their families face have been well documented for decades. Compare current research to research done in the late 90s and you'll see little has changed. Assignees and their families still have the pervasive sense that the 'company' does not understand the real challenges of the relocation process – that they are not appropriately supported. And yet, organizations report they spend too much, costs are always under scrutiny and global mobility professionals are constantly challenged to get more from less.

In this book, Louise and Evelyn propose a solution that is neither complex nor necessarily costly. At its heart it's about understanding perspectives and expectations through open communication. It's time to bring the global mobility conversation back to what matters and makes the difference to the people who live the experience. This means supporting employees to understand the challenges and opportunities of international relocation. This book provides the foundations for an informed decision, which sets realistic expectations about an experience that is life changing and enhancing for both the assignee and, in over 50% of cases, the accompanying partner and family.

The authors aim, through education, to support the relocation process and beyond, ensuring the focus of international employees is where it needs to be and the potential of international assignments is realized.

Louise and Evelyn bring to this book their personal and professional experience of international relocation, jointly equating to over 40 years. They know what it takes to relocate successfully. Their professional work as coaches and their personal lives as expats have brought them into contact with hundreds of globally mobile families. They've researched the expatriate experience. They published their Career Choice and the Accompanying Partner survey report in 2012 based on the input of over 300 expat partners in over 40 countries. Between them they have interviewed human resources and global mobility directors from a variety of companies, including some of the world's largest, and industry thought leaders from academic and consulting disciplines. Louise wrote her dissertation for her master's in occupational psychology on international relocation and adjustment.

Both Louise and Evelyn repatriated back to the UK in 2014 – a coincidence and a move that didn't bring them any closer geographically. Having created Thriving Abroad while living in Lisbon and Brussels respectively, Louise now lives with her husband and two daughters in Hampshire, in the south of the UK, and Evelyn lives with her husband, son and daughter in Scotland (returning to Scotland after 25 years abroad).

While co-authoring the book, Evelyn sadly took the difficult decision to leave Thriving Abroad, the business, for family reasons. Evelyn remains a great friend, support and sounding board as Louise takes the book, its message and the business forward.

How to connect

Find out more about Louise and Thriving Abroad at www.ThrivingAbroad.com. You can also follow Louise on the following platforms:

Facebook: www.facebook.com/ThrivingAbroad
Twitter: www.twitter.com/ThrivingAbroad
LinkedIn: www.Linkedin.com/in/louisewiles